THUS FAR

A Journey From Heartache To Healing
and Hope Trough Christ

TAMMY DANIEL

ISBN 13: 978-0692754818

ISBN 10: 0692754814

Published by Zondervan www.zondervan.com

Cover and Interior design by Vanessa Mendozzi - www.vanessamendozzidesign.com

Contents

INTRODUCTION

Today came with a mix of blessings and questions, but I feel it is time to begin writing down my story . . . thus far. It isn't a beautiful story, but it's mine—the story of what God's grace has brought me through. I am in the middle of the greatest storm I have ever had to face in my life, but it's now when I sense God compelling me to share, with hope that readers can hear my heart and be strengthened on their individual journeys.

It is a wonderful fall day, and I'm sitting at an old picnic table in a beautiful area by a creek on the Natchez Trace. The sun is shining, and the wind is gently blowing. I love this spot. I often come to talk to God and to pray, and I find comfort here. In this place I am truly at peace, and I want to sit here all day.

A huge tree lies broken across the creek, and beside me is another broken into many pieces. Yet in the middle of brokenness I feel at home, for it is here that I am reminded of how God uses brokenness for His good. Watching the water flow, I realize it is unaffected by the tree broken across the bank, or the leaves floating in it, or the weeds growing along the creeksides. The flow continues.

I know God longs for my life to be the same as this creek. I know He longs for me to be flowing for Him, not stopping because of the debris life's storms have left in my way. Ecclesiastes 3:1 states, "To everything there is a season, a time for every purpose under heaven." May God use this season in my life for His kingdom's purposes; and as I put my story "on paper," including how His grace has supported me throughout, I pray my words encourage others.

....

I began to write my life's story about two years ago, but I went back and forth with exactly what God's will for it was. I wanted to be certain I followed what God was asking me to do. Did He want me to write it all down to help me in the healing process? This was a great possibility. I would write and read it, and I knew healing was taking place in my heart through all those months. Was this why God asked me to write my story, for myself only?

I prayed and sought His will. I listened for His voice. But I couldn't find peace about this. For about two weeks, I sensed God speaking to me, telling me to share my story. I was fearful and unsure, but I told God I would do as He asked because I trusted Him.

During this time, I texted a friend of mine whom I rarely text. A few weeks earlier she had invited me to hear her speak, but I couldn't exactly remember when it was. During the text I told her I was going to come. She texted, "Saturday?" I asked, "Like this Saturday?" And she replied, "Yep, like in four days!" I went to hear her speak.

She had no clue about my book or how I had been seeking God about releasing my story. She had no idea what the book was titled, nothing. As I was listening to her speak, she read 1 Samuel 7:12, "Thus far the LORD has helped us."

I sat in amazement. God was using her to speak to me! It was as if a bright light shone over my head, and I heard, "Hallelujah!" She focused on how important it is to share our "Thus far" life experiences to help others. That very moment I told the Lord that I was listening and I would follow Him.

For years I was involved in many areas of ministry yet hid my private life. While ministering for Christ, I became consumed in it all to forget the pain of my home life. But I trust a mighty God whom I now felt called me to be transparent. I really never planned on writing a book. I guess I thought that must require being a professional writer, which I am not. I am only an ordinary woman. I am a *nobody* in one sense. Then I stop and think, *No, I am a child of the King; I am a vessel, just as Paul was, David was, Abraham was, and all the other patriarchs of the Bible. I, too, have a responsibility to my King. He has brought me safe thus far. For kingdom purposes it's time to share the story of my life.*

After the seed was planted in my mind, I sensed God talking to me about my story—showing me that He had given me the boldness I have for a reason, that He knew the course my life would take before I was ever born. Again I thought about the countless stories in the Bible of how God chose to use normal, everyday individuals. After many nights and days of prayer, I decided it was time to write my story. God burdened my heart so that all the pain I have been through has a purpose. Though I cannot see the way ahead, I only need to hear the Shepherd's voice. God called me to tell my story. I heard Him and I obeyed.

I also want to tell about my life to warn of what happens when we let our guard down, when we think we are the last one who will fall. I was saved when I was eight years old in my home and was taught to serve by a loving father and mother. At a young age I began playing the piano for church and have served fervently most of my life. But satan knew where I was vulnerable, and I left a small crack for him to enter. Over time I went from being over the women's ministry in my church and speaking at a women's conference to being divorced and having an emotional affair. You say what?! That is what I say now.

Satan had my eyes covered, but I didn't get there overnight. Now looking back I can see how I let my guard down slowly. How flesh took over. I lost sight of heaven's goals and put my eyes on me. I had four children whom I had raised to love God and follow hard. Now they were watching their mother crumble. Because of my choices, I lost dear friends and much more.

I thought I could handle the feelings and thoughts. I said, "I will never fall." Then I fell hard; I face-planted into the ground. I truly did not think I would ever bounce back. And yet you now have my story in your hands. I did bounce back. I became an overcomer! Grace has brought me safe thus far. His grace has covered me. I know God will use my past for His glory. I am making the choice to let Him use me, all of me. We all have a story of what He has brought us through. Big or little, God wants to use us in His world.

Sharing our stories can help bring healing to our souls, but also it can help others heal. Sharing my story—my thus far—through this book, my greatest desire is to bring glory and honor to Jesus. But part of my prayer is that as you read, Jesus will use my words to bring you hope and the words jump off the pages as a reminder that everything in our lives has a purpose under heaven, that "all things" really do work together for our good and His glory. Finally, I pray as you read that you are reminded how important it is to share your story.

PART 1: MY STORY

Jesus use me, and oh Lord don't refuse me;
Surely there's a work that I can do.
And even though it's humble, Lord help my will to crumble.
Though the cost be great, I'll work for You. (Jack and Billy Campbell)
In Loving Memory of my Father, Clyde Hudson

CHAPTER 1

Childhood

If I am going to tell you my story, I guess I need to start at the very beginning of my life.

Almost 47 years ago (Wow!!) I was born in the home of an old-time preacher. My parents prayed for almost eight years for a child before I was born. Those who know me are probably saying something like: "They were stuck with you after all that prayer!" I have a cassette tape of my dad speaking in a church one night. He prayed, "God, if you will give me a child, I will give that child back to you." From the time I was small daddy had me singing in church. I would stand on top of his guitar case when I was three and sing. I loved to sing. My parents taught me to love the Lord with all my heart, soul, and mind. Dad taught me to serve by singing whenever I had the opportunity. He and my mom sang in church. Dad played his Gibson guitar, and he could really wear that instrument out. He loved it. He always had a huge smile on his face. He knew to whom and for whom he was singing; it was written all over his face. The song I remember he sang the most was "Jesus Use Me." This is the chorus:

Jesus use me and oh Lord don't refuse me
Surely there's a work that I can do;

Thus Far

And even though it's humble, Lord help my will to crumble;
And though the cost be great, I'll work for you (Jack and Billy Campbell).

He boldly proclaimed Christ whenever he was given the opportunity. Dad was very musical and he played the old upright bass in bars before he was saved and that's where I get my deep love for music. But when God saved my dad it was obvious to all who knew him. He wanted to tell the world about the man who changed his life forever.

Sometimes as a kid, I would get a little embarrassed. We might be driving down Main Street in our small town, and dad would roll down his window and just yell to the person on the sidewalk, "Are you saved? Do you know Jesus?" I would want to crawl under my seat. But he was never ashamed to talk about our Lord, I grew up in a home where the gospel was not only taught, but was lived by my parents.

Our life was mostly spent at the church or visiting people from the church or cleaning the church. My dad preached at a church an hour away, so our Sunday was a long day. The roads we drove were curvy, and I got carsick. Every Sunday my mom would say "Look straight ahead." I would try, but eventually we would have to pull over.

It wasn't always pleasant for my father; sometimes it was stressful being a pastor. I watched people yell at my dad and one night a man punched my dad because dad stood for Christ and would not waiver. But mostly the memories are great from our little church. I loved all the people and the time we spent with them.

SINGING AND FAMILY

We would often spend our Saturday nights going to a friend's house to gather around and sing. My dad would take his guitar and there would be a room full of people. We would all sing the old songs. He, my mom and her Aunt Linda sang in a group and would go to sing at churches on many Sundays.

My mom's grandmother would often go with us; Mama Lane or "Mamaw," as we called her. She would wear her long white hair up in a bun and dress in a long skirt, and sometimes a bonnet. She loved the Lord. She would sing the old song, "If anyone makes it all the way home, surely I will" (Albert E Brumley). I don't love the song, but I loved when she sang it because she knew to whom she was singing. I remember one church my dad would go to every year to preach a revival. To get there we had to take a ferry across the river. Mamaw would go with us and sing and listen to the preaching.

While most of my childhood revolved around church, I do remember our family enjoyed playing "Rook." Our family would gather at my aunt's and play until all hours of the night. My dad taught me how to play the game, but I wasn't very patient in learning and got mad several times. If my mom were sitting here with me, she would say that I had that Hudson temper come out in me. I don't know; but either way, I finally learned to play.

Another wonderful childhood memory was when my dad would preach a week-long revival that took place at Ruskin Cave in the rural Tennessee area. The service actually took place in a big cave. We would stay there for the week. It was a fun place to stay with many activities. We had friends who camped and we would all do the activities together. It was definitely the highlight of my summer.

Since I was my parents' only child, they would spoil me with lots of wonderful gifts. I remember getting the colored chickens for Easter, and one year I got a duck. I loved that duck. We would put him in the pool out back and at night put him under our house so nothing would happen to him. One night my niece, who was maybe three or four years old, decided to give the duck a bath in the faucet out back. My mom found her holding the poor duck by the neck. She grabbed him and I am sure I was crying my eyes out because he seemed to be dying. He was just limp in her hands, but she grabbed a blow dryer and he began to come back to life with the warmth from the dryer. Yeah!! Mama saved his little life. We decided after that to take him to Luther Lake in town to leave him so he could be around other ducks. As we left we turned around to see him following behind us. I cried all the way home; so we went back, of course, to get him the next day only to discover he was gone. I didn't really appreciate the things my parents did for me until I had children of my own, and now I understand.

LIFE CHANGED FOREVER

When I was around the age of eight, daddy had open-heart surgery. His heart was physically not in good shape. The doctors told him he couldn't preach anymore. I remember how hard it was for him to give up his church. He longed to be behind that pulpit; preaching the gospel was his passion. He did, however, take any opportunity he was given to speak on occasion for other pastors. I was taught by example to give my all for Christ. I loved going to church. My parents never had the attitude that "Sunday is church and we have to go, okay?" It was that Sunday is the *Lord's day*, the best day of the week; and I was excited to go to church.

On February 17, 1980, my father was given an opportunity to preach at a church close to our home. We attended there at times and were friends with the pastor and his family. We had grown up knowing them and going to singings together. We had family stop by our house that day. I ask Daddy if I could stay home that night with them. I never stayed home from church. But he let me. I remember hugging him before he left. I was a Daddy's girl for sure. I went everywhere with my daddy. He had a spot off the highway where he would go to pray in the woods. He had built an altar there. I loved going with him. Anyway, that night I told him I loved him and they left. He said "I'll see you after church," with that big smile on his face.

I was told that he and my mom sang that night and he played his guitar. Then before he preached, he asked all the youth to line up across the front. They knew by now what he wanted; he wanted everyone to testify. (He thought young people should start early and learn to speak up for Jesus. Of course the teens were horrified at having to do this. But he started at one end and each one said something, even if it was only, "I love Jesus.") On that night after the testimonies dad began to preach. His message was about the Son going home to be with the Father. Suddenly his chest began to hurt. He stopped and said, "We need to pray; I feel like I am having a heart attack." So he knelt down behind the podium to pray and fell backwards.

My father died right there. One moment he was preaching about going to be with the Father and the next moment he was with his Heavenly Father. Nurses in the crowd came and tried CPR and an ambulance was called. A couple stopped by our home to tell us to meet them at the hospital. I remember running up to the ambulance and trying to get to my dad. I could see his long legs hanging off the stretcher. But I was kept back from him. We all went into the waiting area. There were people everywhere. I remember feeling really sick. I went to the restroom and came back and everyone was gone. I walked around a corner and was told my dad had died. I was only ten years old and in shock. I was taken to my mom who was crying. I remember saying, "Mama, Daddy said not to cry if he died; he was in a better place."

I often think about the night my dad died. I know my God loved me so much that He made sure I would not be there to see daddy die. I don't remember ever missing church unless I was sick. I shouldn't be amazed that our God watches over us so closely. He is my good Shepherd. He watches over His sheep. As a child He protected me from watching the man I loved so much leave this world. I hold fast to the promise that one day I will see him again. We will walk and talk forever in eternity.

MISSING MY DADDY

I didn't know how I would make it without him. But he died doing what he loved more than anything, telling about our Savior that he loved with all his heart. God had given my dad one more opportunity to preach His Word. He truly gave his life for Christ. His story is one of redemption. Christ took his sinful life, saved him, and used him to tell of His saving grace.

He instilled in me a deep desire to serve the Lord. My parents didn't wait to teach me the ways of Christ when I got older; they started when I was a child. By the time my dad died, he had shown me by example how to serve. I had watched my parents depend on God. We didn't have a lot of money, yet I remember dad and mom tithing faithfully. And God always provided.

Today as I write this, I miss my dad so much. It's been 36 years but it seems like yesterday. There have been times I have questioned God and asked why dad had to die? I look at the many obstacles that have occurred in my life and wonder why He took my dad. Grieving is a hard process for the young. It's hard to understand at that age that God has a purpose, a plan, for every life. I didn't understand that. I just wanted daddy back. I wanted life to go on as normal. But that was not the plan God had for our family. Now that I am an adult, I wouldn't want to bring him back to this old world. He is sitting at Jesus' feet, basking in the sunlight of His face forever. It's not mine to question God and His ways. I have to accept His timing and be thankful for the time He gave me with my dad. Psalm 139 says, *You formed my inward parts, my frame was not hidden from you. God placed me in the home of Clyde and Wilma Hudson with a plan in mind. It's part of my thus far....*

HE MADE A MARK FOR CHRIST

Last summer I went to play the piano for a funeral. As I walked down the hallway, I recognized the minister. He stopped me and asked if I was Tammy. I said, "Yes, I am." He went on to tell me he was saved under my father's ministry. I was thrilled that God had used this man's life for kingdom purposes. Another day, a lady came up to me at a funeral and shared she also was saved when my dad was preaching. I was so excited to hear this and equally proud to call him my dad. It did my heart good to hear all of these stories. Thirty- two years after his death, his memory is still alive because of what he did for Christ while he was living. What a blessing these two individuals were to me. I knew God had sent them my way to encourage my weary heart or maybe to help me see it is what we do in this life for Christ that matters. Then, I had to stop and think about my own life. Was I letting Christ fully use me? Was I taking every opportunity to tell others about Him? It made me feel very small. It made me think about my story. I had been trying to run from the fact that I felt God's calling on my life. I just didn't see how He could use me in a way other than music. I didn't really want to tell my story either. I would say, "Lord, I am willing, BUT..." There was always the "But, Lord, surely I couldn't be of use." I was convicted by my dad's life, but unwilling to do what God was calling me to do.

MOSES' STORY

As I was writing this I thought about Moses. Who would have thought after his mom put him in a basket that he would survive, much less be used to lead his people out of bondage. God gave him a home in a palace and allowed his mom to be his nanny. Who could do that but our mighty God? Yet Moses felt unworthy for God to use him when God began to speak to him. God said, "I will be your mouth, just go and do as I have asked; I will do the rest." Moses obeyed and look what God did through him. Don't you think Moses had to ponder about why God would use him to lead his people out of Egypt. After all, Moses had murdered a man earlier and fled the scene. Yet God forgave him and used him. He probably expected to live quietly in the desert for the rest of his days. But his "thus far".... was very different. One of my favorite verses is Exodus 14:13: *Stand still and see the salvation of the Lord*. Moses had brought his people to the Red Sea and they thought they were going to die there. How could they get across this water with the Egyptians right behind them? They cried, "Moses, you brought us all this way, now we will die." Then God stepped in and said, "Moses, lift your rod." The sea parted! (Can you imagine walking across a dry river bed while the water is standing right beside you. Wow!) As they went across, verse 25 tells us that God protected them by taking the wheels off the chariots of the Egyptians. I would have loved to have seen that. Psalm 20:7 tells us, *Some trust in horses, but we will remember the name of the Lord!* God is able to accomplish his divine purpose through whomever He chooses. He writes our story. What a story Moses had. He never expected that God would have brought him safe this far…. and keep leading him.

GOD USES OUR STORY

God uses our stories even today. Sometimes satan whispers, "Keep quiet; you will just embarrass yourself if you tell about your life. You don't talk about that kind of thing to other people. Just forget it happened and go on." Satan has whispered that in my ear. But, I am telling him to bug off!! I am stepping out of my comfort zone in faith, knowing God will decide how to use my story.

Are you fully trusting in his grace this hour, as the song says? It might be your neighbor that needs you to open up to her and share Christ. It may be the lady in the grocery store. But God will use your story if you allow Him to. It may seem like a small thing compared to others, but it is your life and your story. God uses everything for His good.

I hope as you finish this chapter you are encouraged to open your mouth and begin to share Christ whenever you can. It may be your last opportunity. My dad didn't expect to die that night, but he finished well, and his story will be alive for years to come. What will your story be when your life is over?

His grace has brought me safe thus far…
And grace will lead me home (John Newton)

Do not merely listen to the word…do what it says. James 1:22

Dear Jesus, thank You for the home You placed me in. I thank You for the parents You gave me, who faithfully taught me of Your ways. I know You had a plan and purpose for my life even before I was ever born. Thank You for loving me! I love You and praise You for all You have given me.

- How did your "thus far" journey begin?
- What kind of childhood memories do you have?
- Did you have a painful childhood?
- What are some of the good childhood memories you have?
- Are you teaching your children the ways of Christ?
- Consider sending your parents a card this week and let them know how much you love them if they are still with you.

Share some of your childhood memories with your small group or a friend. It will be interesting to hear some childhood stories!

Even if your childhood was painful, stop and allow yourself to think back. Pray and ask God to help you through the painful memories. Get your journal out and write them down and this will help you to be able to let go of the pain and heal from the past. If you have wonderful, happy memories, stop and thank God for those. He had a plan for your life, even before you were born. Stop and thank Him for that.

Read Psalm 139 and enjoy thinking back on your childhood.

What is your story? Do you use every opportunity to share Christ? Or, like me, do you say, "God, are you sure you want me to say something?" I have heard so many say, "He is only looking for a willing vessel. He will do the rest." God is waiting to use our stories for His glory. Oh, that we would open our hearts and our mouths and let Him use us.

He set my life to music, He gave me words to sing
He set my life to music, now life's a symphony
From the valleys of my heart, let His praises ring,
He set my life to music, and loves the melody (Dennis W. Morgan and Kyle Fleming)

CHAPTER 2

He Set My Life to Music

After my dad died, my mom had to go to work. She had been a stay-home mom; but we didn't have a lot of money, so she had to find a job. I didn't understand this at the time, but I know now that must have been hard on her. I missed my dad terribly. I began at that time to push my emotions down, not allowing myself to cry very often. I never told anyone how I felt. I just longed for my dad so much. I was only ten years old and didn't understand death. I only knew I missed the man who had loved me and cared for me so much.

MY LOVE FOR THE PIANO

The only thing I did was play the piano. I don't know if you have ever heard this, but most people who play the piano are good in school but sports is not their "thing." Now there are exceptions to this, but I wasn't good at any sports. Playing the piano was my "thing." I loved it. I practiced daily. I poured myself into my music. At the age of twelve I became the full-time pianist for my church.

I had a record player and I would play records and sing to the top of my lungs. Probably drove my mother crazy sometimes! I just loved to listen to music.

My mom always encouraged me to practice. She took me to piano twice a week for lessons. I knew how to play by reading the music and was learning to play by ear. My dad had taught me some about chords, so I began to really work on that.

The pastor of the church my dad had been preaching in when he died would pick me up for church if my mom was working. He and his family lived close, and I would stand at the door and watch for them. They were faithful to take me and bring me home or wherever their family went. They were so good to me.

EMBARRASSING MOMENTS

Their daughter was about six or seven years older than I and eventually I began to hang out with her and her friends. Everywhere they went, I was tagging along behind. She knew how easily I would laugh; so when I would sing in church, she would do something to make me laugh. I remember looking out to see she had drawn eyes and put them in an old pair of glasses and was looking up over the head in front of her where all I could see was the eye balls. Of course I would laugh. One time we were singing in church. We wore these bright green and orange earrings shaped like big bouncy balls. We got each other tickled while we were singing. After we sat down, the man preaching made each of us read Bible verses so we would stop laughing. Of course they made me go first. As I was reading, one friend was pulling on the slip I was wearing under my dress while I read. No one could see her, but it made me giggle. I probably had to read a whole chapter by the time I was through. These crazy girls got me in a lot of trouble at church! I had fun with them though. We always had good clean fun. They were like sisters to me. They made my life very interesting.

One night about six or seven of us girls went to sing at a little community center. An old pastor we had grown up with was preaching and he had asked us to sing. He loved the fact that we loved being in church. He wanted to show us off a little bit. He told the crowd how we loved to sing and be where God's word was taught. I was playing the piano, which had one of those little mirrors across the top. Those got me in trouble every time. I saw one of the girls start to laugh about something and that was all it took. I fell apart at the piano. They could see my face in that mirror. Old Bro. Baggett was playing the guitar and didn't look too amused. One by one the girls were laughing so hard they just began to go sit down. By the time the song was over, Annette was the only one on the stage singing alone. She never quit. It was so funny. We still laugh about that today. I would be so embarrassed if my children did these things! We were awful.

TEENAGE YEARS

I went through those awkward teenage years. I never dated or really even thought about it. I didn't think I would ever get married. I didn't think I was lovable for some reason. I don't know if that is how I dealt with death or what caused me to have that thought about myself.

Years after this I began writing Christian songs. I have always had a deep love for music, especially the hymns for church where I knew them so well. Even now I love to sit and play the hymns and sing those words. There is such strong biblical truth in those old hymns.

I may seem a little old-fashioned, always to begin one's work with prayer, but I never undertake a hymn without first asking the good Lord to be my inspiration
-Fanny Crosby

Writing songs usually is a way to tell about where I am in life. I always smile inside when God begins to place lyrics in my mind. I am always amazed at the timing of these lyrics and then the song that comes from them. Music is a wonderful way to express my love for Christ.

A fun night for me would be gathering a group of friends and singing around the piano. I love it! Hearing all the beautiful harmonies soothes my soul. There is something to be said about getting lost in a song.

Psalm 71:23 My lips will shout for joy when I sing praise to You- I, whom You have redeemed.

HE SET MY LIFE TO MUSIC

I wanted you to know a little about me and my love for music. God gave me this love and I will never cease to thank Him for this talent He bestowed upon me. There are many times I am able to play for a funeral and minister to a family using my hands. That blesses me more than them.

My grandmother was the only other member of my family who played the piano. She played by ear. But I used to watch her hands go up and down the old piano. She gave me the desire to play the piano. I have her upright piano in my piano room and wouldn't take anything for it. I have four pianos in my house, actually five, counting the little piano I still have that I got when I was three. In the basement I have the piano my dad gave me when I was young. Upstairs I have my grandmother's piano, my keyboard, and a baby grand that I was given by some dear people. I love my pianos. I teach piano and love to watch my students' faces light up when they begin to really catch on. It is so exciting for me to teach them. I love it. Several of my students have gone on to play for their churches, and that thrills my heart. I love to be able to ask each one of them about their days and hear where they are in life when they come to lessons. It is such a rewarding job!

My friends often laugh that I have a song for everything. You know how you are doing something, and someone says something and it reminds you of a song or a commercial? We all do that. I just have a little bit of a problem doing it quite a bit! I relate everything to a song.

If I am teaching a Bible study, I often use a song. Music has a way of ministering sometimes more than teaching could. There are so many days during worship service my heart becomes overwhelmed with praise as I lift my voice singing to my Lord. Music touches the soul down deep, stirring you and drawing you into the presence of the King in a mighty way that words cannot express.

Music has been a vital part of my life. When I taught Sunday School we always had music time. The kids loved it too. It often does our heart good to sing those little songs we learned so long ago. I love to hear my kids sing these songs still. There are days I'm working in my home and hear one of my girls singing and playing the piano. It puts a huge smile on my face as I listen to them sing praises to our God.

Yes, Jesus loves me; Yes, Jesus loves me
Yes, Jesus loves me; the Bible tells me so (Anna Warner).

So if I were going to tell you my story, I had to first share with you my deep love for music. Everyone who knows me knows this about me. I love to play the piano and sing. I love Christian music because it soothes the soul. I pray to always not only have a smile on my face, but His song in my heart.

*** Pray * Ponder * Praise ***
Do not merely listen to the word...do what it says. James 1:22

Dear Jesus, thank You so much for the gift of music You have placed in my life. There are so many days I sit down at the piano and sing to You and feel my stress being lifted. I thank You that I can use this gift to encourage weary souls, and at the same time encourage my own. May I always use the ability You have given me to play the piano and sing only in service for You. Lord, help me never forget how important music is to everyday worship. Thank you for the songs that you place on my mind throughout the day that draws my heart to Yours. Thank you how many days my heart is lifted by a song. I love You Jesus. I am reminded that in Zephaniah 3:17, You sing over me! Thank You so much for placing Your song in my heart. I love You Jesus!

- What kind of music do you like?
- Has God given you a special song or songs that remind you of a certain time in your life?
- What influence has music had in your life?
- Do you sing to God when you pray? (I do) If you did, what song would you sing to Him?

Stop and thank God for the beautiful gifts He has given you or others for music. Remember He sings over You. Find some praise music and let Him lift Your spirit with a song.
Read Zephaniah 3:17.

I must tell Jesus, I must tell Jesus, I cannot bear these burdens alone
I must tell Jesus, I must tell Jesus, Jesus can help me, Jesus alone (Elisha Hoffman)

CHAPTER 3

Here Comes the Bride

During high school I worked at a local restaurant to make extra money. There I met my boss! After time, we began dating. I enjoyed spending time with him; he was a fun-loving guy.

After my dad died, I missed the love he had shown me. He was a hugger and was always saying "I love you." My mom was a godly Christian woman but just wasn't a hugger. She didn't grow up with a mom who told her she loved her, so my mom didn't always say, "I love you" or know the importance of saying it. I was craving love.

DATING

He wasn't a Christian when we began dating, but he was a very nice guy who treated me really well. I didn't take him to church or around my friends very much. I did tell him after a date where he ordered an alcoholic drink that I didn't drink and didn't want to be around it. He didn't drink alcohol again. That settled that. He was very loving to me. He would take me shopping and shower with me with nice things. I remember he bought me my very first Liz Claiborne purse and a matching wallet. I was so excited. I had never had anything so nice.

We dated for three months then decided to get married. We were sitting in the parking lot of my church when he asked me to marry him. I never thought I would meet anyone, so I was very happy.

The first time he went to church with me was Easter Sunday. We were engaged! I had grown up in this church, so everyone was trying to figure out who he was. Then they were shocked when they heard we were engaged. My pastor and his brother took me downstairs during Sunday school to try to talk to me about this. I was adamant that I was in love and everything was okay. They were concerned at such a fast engagement. I don't remember everything they said, but I knew they were very bothered.

He went forward that Sunday for salvation. It seemed all was working out. We were married that same year. I couldn't wait to start our life together. I was so happy because I had found a man to love me and cherish me. He was a Christian. It seemed life was perfect.

SOMETHING IS JUST NOT RIGHT

Almost immediately I knew something wasn't right, but I didn't tell anyone. I couldn't put my finger on my concerns; however, I had a strange feeling that something just wasn't right. The affection he had shown me during our months of dating seemed to be gone. Our intimate life wasn't like I thought it would be. I had been reared thinking that I shouldn't talk about private issues in my marriage with others, so I didn't. My friends would talk about their married lives. I would listen but I never said anything. I immediately wondered what was wrong with me. We were newlyweds and I wanted to be a great wife. I wanted to make him happy.

Yet all I knew was that I had a feeling way down deep that didn't feel right; so I would just pray and remain quiet. I went for counseling to try to figure it out. I must not be loveable. I asked him to tell me what I was doing wrong. He would get mad and say nothing. I didn't know what to do so I just kept silent. The pain was beginning to consume my heart.

When I finally began to figure out the issue we had two children. We had built a new home and I had quit my job to be a stay-home mom. In public we were one big happy family, but in private there was so much pain inside me. I felt I was almost living a double life. I love people. I had great friends, and I was very involved in my church in the music program. No one knew that inside I was dying a slow death. I prayed and asked God to show me what was wrong with me. It had to be me.

One night the kids and I had fallen asleep downstairs. I awoke and went to find my husband. I found him in the floor watching television. He had a startled look on his face, so for some reason I took the remote and pushed play. I was in shock. *Pornography*. I didn't know anything about this trash. I only knew it was trash. I had never seen anything like it. I took the video tape and tore it apart and threw it away. I thought that would be the end of that. I didn't tell anyone about it. We talked about it a little, but I had no idea it was an addiction.

THE DEMONS OF PORNOGRAPHY

Things didn't change much in our intimate life. Some nights I would cry myself to sleep because I so wanted for him to desire me. He never said a word. It would make me angry that he didn't seem to care. Sometimes he would hold me as I cried but no conversation. Only I didn't know what was wrong. I had no idea it was because of pornography. I had no idea of the demons tormenting his soul. I had no idea he wanted to quit but couldn't. I had no idea that every day his mind was enveloped by the prince of darkness himself. He wanted to stop but the shame was great. He couldn't do it without Christ. He never told me. I knew something was wrong for years but couldn't ever figure it out because we had no communication. I felt like I was living life alone.

I would keep everything bottled up inside and then I would explode with anger. We would both yell and he would promise me he wasn't doing anything. He would say, "Go look in the car, you won't find anything!" He would make me feel I was dreaming everything up. We would scream and yell, and he would threaten to leave. I would beg him not to and that was the end of the argument. We would get up the next day and go about our day as if nothing had happened.

Now we had three kids and we had our own bridal and catering business, which was consuming me. My husband hated his job and was having panic attacks. He felt that if we opened this business it would eventually take him from his unhappy job. I liked the business, so I agreed. It wasn't all his decision. It was too hard. His panic attacks became more frequent. I had no idea how to handle them. We would be eating out and he would say he felt like he was going to have a heart attack. We would go to the emergency room only to find out that he was hyperventilating. It happened over and over. He began to attend a group at a hospital for panic attacks to see if that would help. It didn't. The business was overwhelming. I taught piano there and ran the business with my husband's help. On many weekends we catered weddings, we were spread very thin. Honestly, I couldn't focus on the business the way I needed to because my life was spinning out of control. We stayed in the business for about two years. But after a while and because of many bad decisions, we walked away.

Now we were not only unhappy but we were financially drowning. I couldn't take the pressure of home life and this. I was very lonely and longed for my husband to want to be with me, to want to communicate with me; I wanted a best friend in him. But that didn't happen. The life of an addict is a self-centered life. I don't think he realized how consumed he was with his addiction. I didn't realize it at the time but it was the cause of his panic attacks. He had no peace anywhere he was.

SUPPRESSING THE PAIN

As long as I would remain quiet and act like nothing was wrong there was no arguing. I was slowly building walls and suppressing our problems. After a while I would become furious and explode. We would argue, but it didn't change anything. If you suppress your life and don't deal with it, then there is no problem. That is how we were living day after day, year after year.

We did have happy times; they weren't all bad. But rather than deal with our marriage, we just lived like nothing was wrong. That doesn't work. My husband didn't see there was a problem, though, so I felt there was nothing I could do. We were living in a nice friendship, living life like our relationship was normal.

One day my car was broken down and I called him at work. It was like it was *my* problem. I was furious. I had a friend take me to his work so I could get the other car. After I left, he began calling me immediately, but I ignored his calls. When I pulled into my driveway, something told me to look in the trunk. I opened the trunk and began to dig through it. I found a paper sack. I was not prepared for what I was about to see. This time the pornography had progressed. It was worse than before. I was literally sick, but somehow took my children inside. He called and I used some profanity. I never talked like that. I was in shock. I felt like my marriage was over. What was I going to do? I had three children. I called my pastor and confessed the words I had said. Then I asked him to go get my husband. I wanted him to have to face someone that he would be ashamed to see.

I will never forget that day. I felt like I was walking in a fog. We went to the church and talked. He made excuses as to why he had bought this filthy stuff. I was disgusted.

I went home with my friend for the night and took my children. The next day he said he would get help and begged me to come back home. I did. For a time our life was so much better.

WHAT I WAS LEARNING ABOUT THIS ADDICTION

We read our Bibles together and prayed. I was so happy. It seemed our marriage was headed in the right direction. This is what I had always wanted. He went to counseling, and I would go with him at times. I had no idea about this addiction. My mind was on overload at all the counselor was telling me concerning pornography. I didn't want to have to listen or discuss these kinds of private issues with anyone.

I had never known there was so much to pornography. A person addicted to pornography doesn't need a spouse. The porn becomes the spouse. I was horrified at what I was learning about this addiction. I felt sorry for my husband, but I was filled with anger and resentment. I had spent so much time trying to fix me when he was the one who needed repair. How could he not tell me? But satan had him captive. Sometimes I think this is worse than drinking or drugs.

He said he felt relieved he had been caught. He told me he had married me thinking that since I was a pastor's daughter it would help him get over the pornography and live a good life. No one can help another get past sin except Jesus Christ. Pornography consumes the mind. Over and over the mind continues playing the pictures and reliving the videos. He was also looking at the Internet sites. We discontinued Internet in our home. I began to take the newspaper at the counselor's advice and cut the bad ads out. We didn't drive through parking lots of gas stations that sold pornography. We quit watching the pageants on television. We took drastic measures.

His counselor had me purchase a book called, *An Affair of the Mind*, by Laurie Hall. This book helped me to understand this addiction so much better. It was an eye opening book for me. I had no idea how bad this addiction was. It helped me understand my husband much better. During this time I also became aware that he had admitted to marrying me because he thought it would fix him, but what I also knew is I had married the first man who showed me any love. I had been craving love for so long. I did love my husband but was not sure now it was the love either one of us deserved.

You can't marry someone hoping it will change you. This doesn't work.

I continued to swallow everything down and never talk about it. If I want to be real in this book, I have to be honest even with myself. All of our marriage problems weren't his fault. I can take blame too. We both had huge issues that we brought into the marriage and never talked about them. Yet the pornography was a driving force that created a wedge that ultimately could not be broken in our lives. Communication is a vital part of a marriage, and we had very little communication concerning the things that mattered in our marriage. Date nights didn't happen much, unless we went out with a group. He wasn't interested in being alone with me. His needs were being fulfilled by pornography.

We never sat on the couch and cuddled, or just held hands. All the things that intimacy brings to a relationship, we were lacking. Inside I was screaming because I so wanted to be loved! I didn't know what to do. Everything I tried never helped. When you have to beg for someone to touch you, love is lost. No woman wants to beg for intimacy; she wants her mate to long to hold her and touch her. I hated how I felt, but I felt trapped and isolated. I had so much to give but he didn't seem to want it!

SATAN WOULD NOT LET GO EASILY

Time passed and I could just sense when the addiction was back. Strongholds are so hard to break. You have to truly and totally depend on Christ to break free of a stronghold and have an accountability partner.

He had for so long read the Bible and really seemed to have changed. But he had not changed; he was still bound by pornography. I didn't know at the time, but he had been working out of town and had driven by a video store where he made the choice to stop and go inside. My husband had been through a hard few months. His father had died only a few months before this. It was devastating to our family. He said the depression from that is what caused him to stop that day. I had no idea. I just knew he was looking at it somewhere, though I couldn't find anything. When I would confront him about it, he would convince me I was the crazy one and he had nothing.

All I knew was that the same symptoms were back in our marriage, so basically I checked out of the marriage. I was living life but not living. I felt ashamed, unloved, and dirty. My husband didn't want me. I felt like I was unworthy to get my own husband to look at me. But then I began to harbor bitterness and anger consumed my heart. The love for him left. I didn't feel sorry for him but felt anger and rage. We never discussed how unhappy we were, until my emotions rose to the surface and there was no pushing them back down. I would yell and ask him what he was doing. He would say nothing. The same response he had given me every time all through the years. I poured myself into ministry and my children.

It was hard for me to hear my friends talking about their marriages. I wanted a best friend in my husband and all the things they seemed to have; I wanted to be loved. I wanted to have my husband come home and be thrilled to see me. I didn't believe divorce was an option. I felt it was best for my family if I stayed in the marriage. I guess I thought my children believed we were happy but they knew. They had parents they never saw hold hands, never saw show each other affection. I would be engulfed in church work while he would sleep or lie around. He was a good father. He always was very loving to the children. But our home life was not normal. I prayed and I begged God to change my husband, and let him walk away from the pornography, but I became discouraged when I saw no change. I guess I decided this was my life and it would never change, so I would just make the best of it.

Now I wasn't going around sad. Honestly, no one knew there was a problem. I had told some close friends but at the time that was it. I loved Christ and the joy of the Lord was my strength. I did trust Him. Yet I felt I was the one who now was to stay in the marriage even if I were to be unhappy forever. I had made a commitment for better or for worse. But I began to doubt God and I became bitter toward my husband because I felt I had no value to him. I didn't see my bitterness as sin; I only saw my husband's sin. It was so easy to be resentful; after all he was into an addiction that had hurt me as well. I would think I had a right to be angry. I dismissed my anger and made excuses for myself. The Bible so clearly talks about getting the stick out of your own eye. This is where I left room for satan to enter my life. Unconfessed sin! It is so easy to say someone else's sin is bigger than mine. How often do we judge others? Sin is sin! The Bible is so clear about this.

SURPRISE! IT'S A GIRL

Many years passed and I became pregnant with child number four. We weren't planning to have any more children, so she was a huge surprise! I was completely shocked that I was having a baby. It seemed that this would be the start of a new chapter. Things were going well. Our other children were much older so it was like starting over! But she was what I felt God had given me during a hard time, a rainbow after the storm. The children were so excited about the new baby. Our home seemed very happy once again. Yet the Holy Spirit was tugging at my heart.

I had that feeling something was wrong several months into my pregnancy. I dismissed the thoughts and would just pray, "Please, God, not again." I just so wanted everything to be okay and for us just to be a family.

The month before my little darling was born; I was looking on the back of his truck and found more pornography. The spirit of God would show me every time. The Psalms speak of God bringing the hidden to light. I prayed often for God to show me if there was something else he was hiding. I sat in my van horrified as I looked through the magazine. I wanted to see what he was reading but it was almost more than I could bear to see. I went into the house and brought him outside and told him what I had found. This time he wasn't sorry but angry I had found it. How could this be happening again? Why now? Not knowing what else to do, I got in my van and started driving. I didn't know where I was going; I just knew I had to get away from him. I had to process what I had just seen and held in my hands.

I ended up at one of my best friend's houses, but I hated to tell her that once again he was looking at pornography. This pornography horrified me! I was nine months pregnant. What was I going to do? I was a stay-home mom. I had no money. I didn't want to tell my family about this addiction. I had never told my mother there was a problem. I decided my only choice and the choice best for my family was for me to stay.

Life moved on. I didn't know if he was still looking at the filth; I was just numb inside. I was going through the motions but had given up on a happy marriage.

After much prayer I decided there is great wisdom in a multitude of counselors. I felt God telling me that in order for Him to use me, I needed to deal with my home life. I began counseling with several friends concerning my marriage and how to save it. I was very nervous talking about such personal issues. But I knew I had to because I needed help. I hoped maybe one of these friends I was counseling with could talk to my husband and God would really use them to help in our marriage. I tried to get him to talk to someone, find an accountability partner, but he refused. Through their counseling, I was able to really share how I felt. I was able to release pain that I had suppressed for some time and I asked one of those friends I was counseling with to call my husband and talk to him. One friend did call him and he went and they met and talked. I didn't know how it went; he never told me, but I was hopeful things would turn around.

I HATED THE THOUGHT OF DIVORCE

For the first time my friends were telling me they thought I should leave. I was really scared. The thought of being on my own frightened me. How would I make it on my own? I had been married since I was 19 years old and now I was much older. I didn't know what to do.

I would think about my children and I just couldn't imagine leaving. The kids had no idea of why I was in counseling, or the problems between their dad and me. They loved the Lord and were so involved in the church and were leaders in their school. I was so proud of them. I knew how divorce would affect them; I just couldn't do it. I felt it would be better for me to live unhappily. I lived under the umbrella that they thought our home was happy. I truly thought this was best for all of us. I knew God hated divorce. That is how I had been taught. I had to make a very hard decision. Would I stay or go? I was so confused and hurting. I had taken vows that said for better or for worse. I had married him, so it was hard for me to talk about divorce. I had godly friends who were divorced. I didn't judge them; I just didn't want that for my family. What was I going to do?

During this time my music became very important to me. I relate everything to a song. Singing and playing the piano was often a way for me to relax and to escape from my life. I would sit and write songs. It was a way for me to talk to God and to say how I felt. A year or so before this I had written a song that God was using to minister to me now. I would read the words over and over.

> *Jesus, You're all that I need, Jesus, You're all that I need*
> *When I think I'm alone in this valley, I feel Your arms 'round me.*
> *In your haven I will stay Lord, I will rest and wait for Thee*
> *For it's here I am learning, Jesus, You're all I need (Tammy Daniel).*

Why did God need this to be a part of my story? How could this possibly help? I didn't want this life in my story. I wanted a beautiful story with a beautiful marriage, just like the fairy tales. Isn't that the story we all want? Prince Charming to ride up and save the day and live happily ever after.

But that is not the story I had. So I would just pray and seek God for the decision I knew was inevitable. *Divorce.* This is not the way I wanted my story to go. I was really angry that this was the life I was living. I know

Thus Far

God writes the story and we are the vessel; I just didn't understand where He was going with MY story. I didn't understand at all.

*** Pray * Ponder * Praise ***

Do not merely listen to the word…do what it says. James 1:22

Jesus, this was a painful chapter for me to write. You know all of the anger and bitterness I held in for so long. I prayed many days for You to break my husband's addiction. Yet I held on to sin in my heart. Thank You for forgiving me and taking away the anger and bitterness I held on to for so long. Thank You for speaking to me about forgiveness and reminding me that I must forgive just as You forgive. I pray now for those who are in a marriage where an addiction has a terrible hold on one of them. Jesus, please help them to come to You and lay down that addiction today as they read this. Help them to know You will go with them through the days ahead; they do not need to fear. I pray for any marriages affected by this that You would guide them to You. Help them to rest in Your almighty hand, knowing You are the only one who has the power to break this addiction. Jesus, I thank You right now for the lives that You are changing and addictions You are breaking. It's only through You we have any hope at all. Be with each weary soul that is struggling in their marriage today. May they fall on their knees and seek Your face this very moment. In Your Sweet Name I pray. Amen

- Describe the communication between you and your spouse.
- Is there something you need to be completely honest with your spouse about that you have been hiding?
- Most couples have had rocky times in their marriages; what is a time when you and your spouse were really having trouble?
- Have you hardened your heart to where you are unwilling to notice the change and efforts made in your spouse?
- Did you resolve these issues alone or with the help of a minister, counselor or friend?
- Have you ever shared this with anyone in hope of encouraging another weary soul?
- Do you or your spouse suffer from an addiction?
- Stop now and ask God to help you seek help for this addiction. Go and talk to someone today who can point you in the right direction.

I have won and I have lost, I got it right sometimes
But sometimes I did not; Life's been a journey
I've seen joy, I've seen regret
Oh and You have been my God through all of it (Ben Glover and Molly E Reed)

CHAPTER 4

The Calm Before the Storm

Life was going on as normal. Days turned to years. I had just given in to the fact that my marriage would never be better than it was at the moment, but I had grown accustomed to the friendship we had. Divorce just seemed so hard for me to think about. I guess I had given up on the possibility of it ever changing. I guess my faith that everyone could see in me, I wasn't demonstrating with my marriage because I really saw no hope of anything changing.

SMILING THROUGH THE PAIN

Inside I was very tired of living a lie. Yet on the outside I was still smiling and living like nothing was wrong. I was praying daily for God to search my heart and show me anything He wasn't pleased with. If you pray that prayer every day with a sincere heart, God will show you. I kept hearing Him say, "Tammy, deal with your life." It truly scared me. I had gotten used to living as we were; and although I wasn't happy, I was content. God seemed to be using me. My husband was content the way life was, so I tried to be too. But if you are a Christian you know what I mean when I say God was tugging at my heart. I knew I had to listen and obey.

I didn't see that very soon I was going to take a sudden turn that would forever change the course of my life and plunge me into one of the darkest times I had ever been in. I didn't see satan weaving his web. I wasn't looking for anything. I had never considered or wanted to talk to another man; it had never been a temptation for me. I had several friends, as I stated earlier, that I was counseling with on my marriage. One of the friendships that started innocently on my part seemed a safe place to share my heart. The depth of his conversation and attentiveness opened up in me something I had never experienced before. In my vulnerable state, I missed some dangerous red flags when he began to open up and share some unmet emotional needs he had in his own life. This was so significant because no one had ever met these needs before now. I didn't realize it at that time, but satan was slowly drawing me into his clutches. I had in times past taught the women about guarding their hearts and what that meant. I had no idea that I was the one letting my guard down. In reality I was in denial and not willing to see that a long time ago I had already let my guard down. Satan had found my weakness. I wanted what every woman wants, to feel loved and appreciated and beautiful, and this friend made me feel all of those things. We were in the beginning stages of an emotional affair.

I read somewhere that you can push your life down for so long, but eventually it's going to come up and out. I began to experience this. I began to talk to others about my husband's problem. I had been silent for so long, but suddenly I wanted to tell. I was tired and crying out for help. It didn't bother me that I was sharing private things with others. I was tired of living the lie.

GOING THROUGH THE MOTIONS

Time passed by and I guess I was just going through the motions. I now look back in utter amazement. It's kind of like looking down on your life and asking what did I just do. Really was that me? How did I get here? It's like one day I was happily leading Bible study and the next I was at home sobbing asking myself what happened. I was totally caught up in an emotional affair. I kept saying I haven't done anything! Yet I knew better, I knew I was ignoring all the warnings God had placed before me. You try to lie to yourself and say "Well, there is no sex, so there is no problem."

WHAT IS AN EMOTIONAL AFFAIR

Emotional infidelity is any relationship that occurs outside of one's primary relationship, where the communication focuses on fulfilling intimate emotional needs, sharing vulnerable things, and receiving validation from that person. (Marina Voron, LMFT)

So when you find yourself excitedly checking your email or your Facebook to see if he or she messaged you, just be honest with yourself; is this just a friendship, or an emotional affair? Today with so many social media platforms, it's easy to find yourself in an intense conversation that's honest, trusting, and revealing with someone you don't even know very well. (Melissa Bykofsky)

I want to give you some signs to look for to know if you or one of your friends is having an emotional affair.

1. **You keep this friendship a secret**. *Would you tell your partner or other friends about all aspects of this friendship? Would you allow anyone, including your spouse, to read your texts/emails with this friend? I read this, "Secrecy is the marker crossing the boundary from friendship to more intimate feelings that could lead to an emotional affair." (Marina Voron)*
2. **You can't wait to talk to him/her because they make you feel alive again**. *The amount of time you communicate would seem excessive to others. We communicated hours most days. They give you the feeling of being alive, something has been awakened in you that you didn't even know was there.*

3. **You realize he/she is on your mind a lot of the time**. *"The more you think about the person, the stronger the feelings are. "(Seth Meyers, PsyD)*
4. **You wish your spouse was more like him/her**. *Any kind of affair begins when there is an unmet need in your marriage. My husband never told me I was beautiful and he rarely touched me, so I didn't feel beautiful. Emotional affairs can begin because you feel neglected by your spouse.*
5. **You share deep feelings**. *You seek out private time together just to talk. This is what ties your soul together, sharing feelings with each other, either online or in person.*
6. **You feel guilty about your friendship**. *You are convinced you are doing nothing wrong because nothing physical has happened, but unconsciously you feel guilty for betraying your partner, which usually means an affair is happening.*

I am sure there are many more signs, but these are the ones that I found true in my situation.

Our conversations at first were all about my marriage, but they soon turned to very personal conversations. I felt he understood me better than anyone ever had. I loved spending time with him.

STATISTICS AMONG CHRISTIANS HAVING AFFAIRS

I read these statistics in an article from *HealthResearchFunding.org (Mar21,2015) 20 Important Emotional Affair Statistics:*

1. An additional 20% of married couples are dealing with emotional affairs above the statistics for physical infidelity. About 35% of wives and 45% of husbands report having emotional affairs, according to the American Association of Marriage and Family Therapy.
2. 22% of men and 13% of women have cheated in their lifetimes, whether they were married or not.

3. Up to 60% of all marriages will deal with at least one form of infidelity over the lifetime of their marriage.
4. When couples are under the age of 30, they are at the highest risk of experiencing an emotional affair.
5. About 3% of children that are born today are as a result of infidelity, which often starts as an emotional affair.
6. Unless it is admitted, the vast majority of emotional affairs are never disclosed to a spouse. Most of the time it is because emotional cheating isn't seen as "real" cheating.
7. Although men are more likely to have an affair, women are more likely to have a long-lasting emotional connection because of the affair.
8. In a recent survey, 88% of women said that they cared more about emotional infidelity than physical infidelity.
9. 56% of men who have affairs claim to be happy in their marriages.
10. More than 60% of affairs start at work. Most people will have an emotional affair with someone that they know.
11. It is not uncommon for a marriage to experience more physical intimacy when one party is engaging in an emotional affair.
12. 48% of men rated emotional dissatisfaction as the primary reason they cheated.
13. 2 out of 3 men felt guilty about having an emotional affair.
14. Only 8% of men say that their primary motivation for having an affair was that they were sexually dissatisfied.
15. Even when physical infidelity occurs, 3 out of 4 men spend at least a month developing an emotional connection before having sex for the first time.
16. Only 34% of women who had affairs were happy or very happy in their marriage.

These statistics are staggering to me. What seems like a harmless romantic longing turns into an emotional affair, which can be damaging to your marriage and your emotional health.

I read in a *Today's Christian Woman* that 55% of women will have an extramarital affair by the time they are forty. Dave Carder's and Duncan Jaenicke's book, *Torn Asunder: Recovering from Extramarital Affairs*, noted that being a Christian doesn't lessen our chances of having an affair. There were three types of affairs they talked about that Christians normally fall into.

3 TYPES OF AFFAIRS

Class One was a one-night stand. Class Two starts as a friendship and grows primarily because of a deficit in the marriage. These often have a powerful emotional connection and involve a shared task or orientation, such as a common ministry or a shared passion. Usually they happen in a marriage where there is little spousal interaction. Sometimes the couple becomes vulnerable after the children are grown and leave. These authors state that emotional affairs are very secretive and powerful influences. People usually insist they've done nothing wrong because no sex was involved. Class Three involves sexual addiction. This is among professing Christians today. That seems shocking, doesn't it? Yet I can understand it now. I am part of that survey. I was a leader, but that did not exempt me from being tempted. I share these numbers to show you how easy it is for Christian people to find themselves in sinful situations. Although I didn't have a sexual affair, what I had done was just as bad. I was a married woman talking to and spending time with another man. I knew better.

WHEN JESUS WAS TEMPTED

The Bible has so many verses about temptation. Jesus himself knew about temptation. Matthew tells us the story of satan tempting Jesus three times. When Jesus was very hungry after fasting for 40 days and 40 nights, that was the moment satan came to tempt Him. He said to Jesus, *"If you are the son of God, then command these stones be turned into bread."* (Matthew 4:3) But Jesus was strong and didn't yield to the temptation; rather, Jesus quoted scripture, *"Man shall not live by bread alone but by every word that proceeds from the mouth of God."* (Matthew 4:4) Satan didn't give up that easily. Jesus just kept quoting scripture. He said, *"You shall not tempt the Lord your God."* (Matthew 4:7) The third time satan tempted Jesus, Jesus said, *"Away with you! You shall worship the Lord Your God, and Him only you shall serve!"* (Matthew 4:10) Then the devil left him alone. So Jesus knew how it felt to have satan come at him again and again. There were many other times in scripture that Jesus dealt with temptation. He knows where we are. I Corinthians 10:13 tells us, *No temptation has overtaken you except such is common to man; but God is faithful, who will not allow you to be tempted beyond what you are able , but with the temptation will also make a way of escape, that you may be able to bear it.* A friend reminded me that God had made several ways for me to escape, but I chose not to take them. She was right. I chose to look the other way when others were telling me to run. People who love us can see what we can't see and we should listen when they speak. I believed I was in control. God did not lead me into temptation; satan did. I could have conquered this and escaped so many times, yet I stayed and dabbled in sin. Look where it took me. I am so bothered when I read James 1:12, *Blessed is the man who endures temptation.* I gave in rather than enduring. Although I know God has forgiven me, it breaks my heart that I did not endure.

BATTLING WITH THE HEART

I let myself trust in flesh rather than God. Now I don't mean that I had a sexual affair, but I just craved being with him, whether on the phone or in person. Sex was not what I wanted; it's the communication I craved. I felt beautiful after so long feeling unloved. I felt alive inside for the first time in years, and I liked the way I felt.

I was involved in a weekly Bible study during this time. I would go and listen but still couldn't give the relationship up. There was such a battle going on in me, such strife within my soul. The Bible tells us in Jeremiah 17:9, *The heart is deceitful above all things, and desperately wicked; Who can know it?* That is where I was. I let my guard down along the way. I allowed sin to enter my life. I heard God's Word every week, but I wasn't listening. I wasn't following God's ways, the ways I had been reared to know. Though my life was a huge mess, I finally felt like I had value to someone. It was a good feeling, so nothing else seemed to matter.

When my life began to fall apart, I wanted to blame everyone or anyone but myself. Yet I knew that my choices had brought me here. So many lives were affected by my choices. I hid in sin for a season. I thought I was living a secret life, but I guess when I saw friends, my face said it all. I felt the weight of where I was in life. Yet I was so involved that I was willing to give up anything.

When it did come to an end, I was a basket case. I wasn't ready for it to end. Honestly, would there have ever been a good time? I was in shock. I felt like I had been run over by a big convoy of semis. My heart was breaking. I totally trusted my friend and never expected him to hurt me even more. How did I expect to flourish in a sin? Yet I did. I was so blind. I didn't know how to live. What was I supposed to do now? When you are enjoying sin, you never think ahead to the end. You live in the moment, thinking a fairytale will last forever. Anything that does not honor God will not last!

I FELT HOPELESS AND SO ALONE

I considered taking my life. I couldn't believe what I had done. Yet I wanted that life. I was very confused. I felt hopeless and angry and so alone. I was in a mess that I had created. My choices had taken me here, yet I was so very sad. I couldn't think about anything else. I was emotionally having a break down. This was too big for God to fix. I just wanted *him* back, I didn't want to go on without *him*.

I found two bottles of pills in the cabinet and I stared at them for hours. I had lost my dearest friends because of choices I had made. I had never felt so much pain as I did at that moment. I didn't know how to get past such devastation and depression. For months I had been in hiding. The public woman was now hidden away because of the shame I felt.

My children were going through so much at this point. They had to deal with the fact that their home life was changing, and their mom had something bad going on and they weren't sure what it was. I did finally talk to my older children, and tell them what I had done, and asked for their forgiveness.

I remember one day walking by one of their rooms, and I heard them crying. When I went in, my child was angry at me and the other party. He saw that I had been very hurt and his anger was overflowing. My children were hurt not only by my actions, but the whole situation. It was agonizing to watch my children suffer because of my choices.

I love to read, yet I couldn't concentrate on a book long enough to remember where I was or what had happened. My family had no idea what had happened to me. I had to force myself to go spend time with my mom. I know she could see so much pain, yet she never asked what was wrong. I hated going out; I just wanted to get home where I felt safe.

I didn't see that life was worth living anymore. I had hurt so many people, and I had been hurt. I couldn't fix it this time. I thought about taking my life with a huge knife one night. But I would picture my little girl and I just couldn't. I didn't see a way out. I had lost my faith and trust in the almighty God. I was focused on the storm. This storm was too big and there was no way out. I felt this would be my defining moment for the rest of my life.

I will never forget one of my sweet friends calling to tell me her brother had committed suicide. He was a pastor who had been in an affair with a young lady in his church. For over a year they had hidden this affair. Then it became public. He and his wife were trying to work things out. He had three precious boys to rear. To dull the pain, he began to drink and take pills. He couldn't live with what he had done. He was so sorry he had ever had the affair, yet it seemed his life was hopeless. He called his sister several times and she would try to give him scripture to help him see that Christ could help him with the past. Yet in his mind, it was a defining moment. Although I know he was a man of faith, he lost his focus for a time. He put his eyes on the storm. In the end, he chose to end his life. I watched my dear friend and her family suffer as a result of his death. Yet now I understood how he must have felt to believe himself so hopeless he didn't want to live. His pain was so great. I too understood that pain. Yet, I couldn't follow through with it. I couldn't give up on life.

BEING TOTALLY OVERWHELMED

Every part of my life was completely turned upside down. I was totally overwhelmed with life. It was too much for one person to endure at the same time. I was so angry! I wanted to hurt those who had hurt me, yet I was only hurting myself. I had forgotten God's ways and was reacting out of pain. I did this for months. I would say I wanted to trust God, but I was taking revenge into my own hands. I hated my life. I didn't want to be with people. I didn't want to go out with my children. I just wanted to sit with my pain. I was having a pity party big time. I thought I was the only one who had ever endured so much pain. I had never felt so hopeless. But I had never been so focused on myself either. I had always, even in a painful marriage, focused on Christ and serving. For the first time I was totally focused on me and my pain. I had so many people trying to help me but I didn't want help. I wanted to feel the pain. At this time, I didn't see it was un-confessed sin that had led me to where I was. I only saw the pain I was in. I wanted to die. Death seemed better than life. I would pray and ask God to please to give me a heart attack to stop the pain. I felt the children would be fine. My husband was great with them. I hated facing the public. I just wanted to fall asleep and never wake up. I drove one day to a secluded area and I took pills with me. I wrote notes and tried to take the pills. But I couldn't follow through. I just didn't think I could move past the pain this time. I was angry on every side. I felt like I was in a horrible pit and I didn't see a way out. At the time I wasn't sorry for my sin; I was still caught up in sin. I didn't care about anything except the love I felt was gone. Nothing else seemed to matter. I would receive kind notes with scripture, but I didn't seem to care. Had it not been for four or five wonderful ladies and the prayers of many others I would never have made it. During this time I had no idea how my family was suffering. I was too consumed with my own pain.

THE WOMAN WHO MET JESUS AT THE WELL

I often now think about the biblical story of the woman at the well and the woman caught in adultery. The woman at the well had been married five times and the man she was living with wasn't her husband. She came to the well at the hottest part of the day. Most filled their jugs at sunrise and sunset. I can imagine she came at this time to avoid people. They were probably all talking about her and how she was living. She was going through all these relationships because nothing filled the void in her life. She was just living but not truly happy. I could relate to her in a way. I avoided people and was running from God. But the story doesn't end there. Jesus happened to come to the well one day. We know it wasn't an accident. Even though Jesus was a Jew and she was a Samaritan, Jesus didn't care, He didn't care that she was a social outcast. He knew about her life. He began to tell her about her life. He said, *"You have been married five times and the man you are living with now is not your husband."* (John 4:17) It scared her because He knew. Can you imagine trying to avoid people, and suddenly a man tells you everything you had ever done? Her heart must have been beating out of her chest. I am sure she began to really listen to Him. He offered her living water that day. After that she felt the void in her heart being filled with Jesus Christ.

Immediately she ran to tell everyone what Jesus had done for her. She didn't care what they thought about her anymore; she just wanted to tell them about the man who had changed her life. I love that story. She found Jesus at the well. He filled her with living water that day. What a testimony she now had to tell everyone. Her life changed forever that day.

THE WOMAN IN THE BIBLE CAUGHT IN ADULTERY

John, Chapter 8, tells us about the adulteress. Israel's law prohibited adultery. Anyone caught in adultery suffered death, male or female. In this story the couple was caught in the middle of the act. The man went free, but the woman was taken to Jesus, who had been in the temple teaching. Thrown before Jesus, with her head hanging in shame, her captors began to ask Jesus about stoning her, wanting her to be put to death. After Jesus listened, He said, *"He who is without sin among you, let him throw a stone at her first."* (-John 8:7) One by one, the Bible says, the people went out, and the woman was left standing there, afraid to take a breath at this point. Jesus looked at her and said, *"Where are those who accused you? Is there anyone here to condemn you?"* She said *"No one Lord."* (John 8:10-11) Jesus said, *"Neither do I condemn you; go and sin no more."* (John 8:11) Can you imagine her shame? She was brought not only to Jesus but there was a crowd there listening to Jesus teach. This all took place in front of many people. Yet there had to be relief that flooded her soul as her Lord didn't condemn her for her sin but forgave her. She never had to feel the shame again; she was forgiven. What a picture of the grace Jesus bestows on us. Her sin was never thought of again; Jesus began to teach to the crowd again, not even mentioning what had just happened in front of them. I feel for this lady; I know how she felt.

I felt so much shame for what I had done. It was hard for me to go out. I carried the weight of what I had done on my shoulders every day. I thought every person I faced whether at the grocery story or at a restaurant all knew about my life, and I felt dirty and ashamed. After time and much prayer by friends I began to crawl out of the hole. I still was not giving all to God. I was saying I was trusting, but I was still trying to manipulate and control the situation. I wasn't following God's ways. As a dear sweet friend always pointed out to me, I wasn't good at accepting "no" or situations I couldn't control.

I was going to counseling which was a huge blessing. Without my counselor each week I would not have made it. She let me know I wasn't crazy but just in so much pain that no one could understand. I could really talk to her and it felt good. I would leave there, having cried the entire time, grieving over the loss in my life. I had a huge problem with trust now and was scared to trust anyone. I was hanging on for dear life to the friends I had. It took months of going to finally see a change. I didn't realize how tired I was, not only physically but emotionally. I would sit at home and go over everything in my mind again and again. It took all of my emotional energy. My counselor was the highlight of my week. She helped me so much. Seeing a good Christian counselor was the best decision I had made in a long time. It led me to emotional freedom as she showed me how to begin to heal emotionally from all I had been through. I finally laid the past down. For a while I felt God moving in my life again. I felt His presence and His peace like I hadn't in months.

NO MORE RUNNING FROM DIVORCE

My husband decided he wanted a divorce during this time. I never expected to end up in divorce. Most people thought the divorce was due to my situation; they had no idea all that I had lived through for years. I was not in a good state of mind. As we went through divorce we lived in the same home because I had no money to make it on my own. I felt so bad for my mom to know I was getting a divorce. She had no idea there was ever a problem until now. I felt I had really let her down. I never wanted to be a divorced woman. I was worried about my children and how this was affecting them.

For so long I had not thought of their needs and what they were going through. Where had my mind been? On me!

I still remember the day my husband moved. It was a hard day for all of us. I knew it was best, but I still remember my children walking out the front door. We were all in tears. I had not been alone since I was 19 years old. The walls were closing in quickly.

The place I was in had awakened a desire I had to be loved that I hadn't felt for years. My flesh was craving to feel loved. I really wanted to find someone who could love me. Yet I knew that would be a bad decision, and I had already made so many bad decisions. Yet I did it anyway. I began to go on dates thinking each man was going to fill that emptiness inside of me. Finally I was going to feel the love I had been craving for so long. I was headed down a bad road that led to more and more pain.

I had found a good church and was going each week. I was hearing great messages. I was determined I could date and be a Godly woman. But it wasn't working out for me. It was too soon; I was very afraid of being hurt, yet I longed to be loved. I realized at this time that my mind was focused on my flesh. I was not following God's ways. These men would never fill the hole in my life that only Jesus could fill.

As I sat at home in utter amazement that I was still bound in sin, I fell on my face and cried out to God. My life was a mess. I was living so far from God. I began to tell God things I hadn't asked Him to forgive me for before. Our pastor had preached about sin the week before and it had convicted me. The Holy Spirit was working on me. A man who spoke the week before had talked about telling God our most intimate secrets. That demonstrated our intimate relationship with God. I had never quit praying. I would cry and tell God I know what I am doing is wrong but I was still not obeying Him.

YIELDING EVERYTHING TO JESUS

I was at a turning point. I knew I was not living in obedience, and conviction was flooding my soul. Jesus pursued me with a vengeance. His Holy Spirit was speaking to me, calling me back to Him. I realized I needed Jesus like never before. It was like a Father longing for His child to come back home. I was the story of the prodigal son. With tears streaming, I sat down at my piano and began to sing, "I've wandered far away from God, now I'm coming home. The paths of sin too long I've trod. Now I'm coming home. Coming home, coming home; nevermore to roam. Open wide Thine arms of love. Lord I'm coming home. (William J. Kirkpatrick). I began to feel the chains fall and the pain being released. I didn't have a job at the time and wasn't sure what I would do, but I felt totally dependent upon God once again. I knew that I had to trust Him like never before. I could see how in the past I had prayed but tried to manipulate the outcome. I had said I was trusting but wasn't totally trusting. I wasn't reading God's Word as I had in the past. So now even though I was in a valley again, I felt happier than I had in years. He knew what I needed to draw me to Him.

My dear friend would tell me she hated watching me jump off the same cliff over again, but she kept praying and sticking by me. She and many others would encourage me daily to trust. I knew it was time for me to truly trust.

I had some decisions I was praying about. At one point I began to worry and wanted to call and get a friend to help but I stopped. I would say, "No, God is in control. I am trusting the almighty God to give me something better than I could have hoped for." I needed to find a job that would pay enough for me to provide for my children and pay my bills. It seemed this wasn't happening quickly and I began to feel anxious. Each morning as I prayed, God began to fill my heart with His sweet peace. He reminded me that He would provide the perfect job in His perfect time. It was like He was bringing me out of the darkness and into His marvelous light. God took my anxiety and replaced it with sweet peace. He was redeeming my life!

PAULS'S STORY OF GRACE AND REDEMPTION

I love the story of Paul, a story of grace and redemption. Yet isn't that what all of our stories are? Why did God place the story of Paul in the Bible? He could have just begun telling how He was using Paul, yet he tells us who Paul was before. As Saul he killed Christians. He had to be filled with such anger, yet God chose to save him and use him. Saul was on the road to Damascus when, as the Bible tells us, a bright light suddenly began to shine all around him. He fell to the ground, blinded by the light. Then all of a sudden, he heard a voice saying, *"Saul, why are you persecuting me?"*(Acts 9:4) Can you imagine Saul's amazement? He had to be shaking with fear, the one who had been so mean to so many. Saul said, *"Who are you, Lord?"* Jesus said, *"Yes, it is I, the one you have been persecuting."* (Acts 9:5) At this point Saul was scared. Finally he was ready to listen. He began to tremble and said, *"Lord, what do you want me to do?"* (Acts 9:6) So he told him to go into the city and he would tell him what to do. There was one problem as he stood up to walk away, he had no eye sight. God had taken his sight for three days. God speaks to Ananias, another of His disciples, and tells him where to go to find Saul. Ananias said, *"Lord, I have heard about this man. He kills people like me. He has great authority. Are you really sure you need me to go and talk to him?"*(Acts 9:13) Ananias was scared to go. I can understand why. Paul was known for his violence toward Christians. But God told Ananias that Saul was his chosen vessel. So Ananias did as God asked him to do. He went to Saul and placed his hands on him and told him what Jesus had asked him to do.

GOD CHANGED HIS LIFE

Saul, whose name was changed to Paul, was filled with the Holy Ghost that day. He was forever changed. What once was a life as a tormentor became a servant of Jesus Christ. I love that. God loves us so much! What a story Paul had to tell as he went from town to town sharing what God had done for him. Can you imagine sitting in the crowd as he told that he was the one who had killed people for speaking as he now was, that he was against God. But this God changed his life and now Paul wanted to tell all people what He had brought him from. Paul had such a story and so do you and I!

I have a lot of junk, a whole lot. Yet, God wants to use my junk to bring Him glory. I am bouncing with excitement, knowing He has something or someone He needs for me to reach with my story of grace and redemption. I can't wait. Can God take shame and regret and turn it around? You bet He can!

COULD THE STORM BE MY GREATEST BLESSING

I read in my devotion book that, instead of having a negative response to trouble in life, I should view difficulties as blessings in disguise. I love the song, Blessings. It reminds me that there is a purpose for everything we go through, even the sleepless nights and tear filled days. I feel as though God is giving me a second chance, just as He did Jonah. Read in the Bible the story of Jonah. He didn't obey God the first time, but after Jonah repented, God gave him a second chance. Like Jonah, this time I am getting it right. I am not going the other way. No way! I have spent too much time in the belly of the whale. I want to be a light shining on a hill, a city that cannot be hidden. I want to tell this world about Jesus who saves us and heals us and gives us second chances and third chances. Amen!

What He needs is for me to share my life with others, the life He gave me. I don't believe any pain has happened without a cause. I could never endure anything compared to what He endured. I am determined to live a life pleasing to Him. I don't need a man to meet my needs and to feel loved. I have my God who loves me unconditionally. He is all I need. He has been waiting for me to seek Him and Him alone. I am content to just love on my children and get my life in order. I have been studying His Word as I did in the past. It is wonderful. I am focused on where I can minister once again rather than looking inward at myself.

I will carry the scars of the past forever, but they will only be a reminder of the grace of God that brought me through. I know my part in my pain and I take full ownership of it. There are consequences to sin and I am reaping them. But there is reward in serving. I am looking upward, focused outward not inward. I serve a risen Savior who needs me to tell others of His unconditional love. He needs me to help others through their pain with my story, a story of grace and redemption through Christ.

Blessed be the God and Father of our Lord Jesus Christ, the Father of mercies and God of all comfort, who comforts us in all our tribulation, that we may be able to comfort those who are in any trouble, with the comfort with which we ourselves are comforted by God. II Corinthians 1:4

WHAT HAS GOD BROUGHT YOU THROUGH

We each have a story. What has God brought you through? I want to use my life to make a mark for Christ. I want to be His hands and feet. I read in Psalm 55, the end of verse 18, *He has redeemed my soul in PEACE from the battle that was against me.* Today I can tell you I have such peace, peace I haven't felt for so long. The battle isn't over but I have surrendered my all to Christ. I can sit back and let him handle the rest. I am not proud of the way I handled myself during this storm. I said and did many things I regret, reacting to the pain and the sin which engulfed me. I will deal with the consequences of those choices for a long time.

What is your story right now? Like me, are you at a place to surrender or will you choose to keep on in the flesh? You are maybe at a crossroad as I was. If I could go back I would have listened to the many people who were telling me I was about to make some bad choices. I have learned when Godly people warn you, listen. I can't go back, but that is perfectly fine because life is about today!

The Calm Before the Storm

I am writing this to make you think about the road ahead. The road your flesh wants you to travel will only lead to pain and regret. Take the other road even though your own heart may be saying no. Take the road to Christ. Don't go by how you feel; go by what is right. You won't have to suffer the consequences or regrets that I have. God will forgive you of anything you have done. I have that assurance and so do you, but there are regrets along the way that I will live with forever. Give the battle to Christ today. Let Him write the rest of your story. He will not only use what you have just gone through, but He will give you a greater story. I pray you will stop what you are doing right now and fall on your knees and beg God to hide you in the shelter of His wings.

I began life in the home of a pastor who prayed for a child and gave that child to God. I still hear my dad's voice in my head, "God, if you will give me a child, I will give that child back to you." Now that child has wandered far away from God and done things she will never forget. That statement my father made more than 40 years ago rings in my ears so often. He taught me a life of obedience to Christ. I have just gone down the road of diso-bedience. I can never go back, but I can go forward. I am redeemed. I am smiling as I type this. I am not proud of the story I just told you; but for the next part of my life, I will tell this story to help others find their way, and as the verse above states, I will help comfort others with the comfort I received from my heavenly Father.

Twas grace that taught my heart to fear
And grace my fears relieved (John Newton)

*** Pray * Ponder * Praise ***

Do not merely listen to the word…do what it says. James 1:22

Jesus, I love You and thank You for loving me despite how I let You down. You remind me in scripture there is no condemnation in Christ. Once I confessed my sins to You, You buried them as far as the east is from the west; You will never remember them again. Thank You for Your grace and mercy. I didn't deserve a second chance, yet You gave me one. You pulled me from a horrible pit and placed my feet back on the rock. Thank You for deliverance. I pray for those who have fallen into sin that they would cry to You for help today. I pray that Your Holy Spirit will show them where they are and show them they need You. I know satan is just waiting to see a weak spot in us, and he found mine. I thank You for showing me that greater is He that is within me than He that is in the world. You break the power of sin. I fell but You picked me up and placed me in Your loving arms. I pray for whoever might be reading this right now and be in the same place that they would get on their knees and beg You to forgive them, knowing You are just waiting for them to ask. Help them know there is no shame; they can hold their head up high. Help them Jesus to take this first step today, right now. I thank You in advance for the work You are doing in their heart and life this very moment. I thank You, my sweet Lord, for dying for my sin and I know if there had only been me, You would have died for me. Thank You for calling me out of the darkness into Your marvelous light. I love You, Lord. In Your sweet name I pray. Amen

- Are you or do you know someone in an emotional relationship?
- As you read this, are you in a friendship that you know you shouldn't be in? Do you see some of the signs of an emotional affair in this friendship?

Please walk away today. Stop whatever you are doing, and get on your knees, and talk to Jesus, and tell him where you are, and let Him help you to walk away right now.

- Describe a time when you fell into sin.

- What weak spot did satan find in you?
- Are you battling the shame you feel from the sin in your life?
- What do you need to lay at Jesus' feet today?

Write it down right now on a piece of paper or index card. Now pray over this.

Hand your shame and regrets to Jesus right now. Do not pick them back up. He wants you to give whatever sin you fell into to Him, never to be picked up again. Now thank Him for taking this sin from you and get up and walk away! Do not pick it back up.

Now rip your paper up and walk away! Do this daily if you need to. Eventually you will leave it forever!

Psalm 103:12, *As far as the east is from the west, so far has He removed our transgressions from us.*

Psalm 107:6, *Then they cried to the Lord in their trouble, and He delivered them out of their distresses.*

This next part of the book I want to use to tell you about the emotions I went through during this season of my life. I want you to know whatever you are feeling is okay, and to know you are not alone. I just told you the story of where life has taken me, so now I want to take you through my journey of healing from the past.

Healing is a process. I have scars from the past and many days these wounds resurface, but I want to share with you how to get past your past once and for all, and how to find joy after the storm.

WEEPING MAY ENDURE FOR THE NIGHT,
BUT JOY COMES IN THE MORNING.
PSALM 30:5

PART 2: HEALING FROM THE PAST

When peace like a river, attendeth my way
When sorrows like sea billows roll
Whatever my lot, though hast taught me say
It is well, it is well with my soul (Horatio G. Spafford)

CHAPTER 5

This Wasn't Supposed To Be My Life and I Am Angry

It's been some time since this storm took place in my life. Yet even today as I read parts of my story I feel my temperature rise! I had a lot of anger to deal with in the aftermath. Anger is a valid emotion, and I believe from reading God's Word that He understands because he tells us to be angry and sin not. But as Christians we can't let anger control us. John Piper says this: "An ongoing, unforgiving, bitter, and angry spirit will kill a person's heart, making them shipwreck their faith…God is showing you how serious this sin is." That's where I was.

FILLED WITH ANGER

I wasn't only angry at what I had just been through. I had been filled with such animosity for so long. I realized I had probably not dealt with emotions from childhood. I was mad that my dad had died. As a child, I didn't know how to deal with death. As a young adult I had never felt loved. I had never talked to anyone about the emotions I was feeling inside. I was mortified with my husband at the way he treated me. I wanted a normal marriage; I didn't want the one we had. Then there was the hurt from the emotional affair. So I layered that on top of all the other anger. Before long, my hostility was spilling out into every part of my life and when left undealt with it, it began to turn to bitterness. Bitterness will spread like cancer through all areas of your body. The Bible links bitterness with being in bondage to sin. "I see that you are full of bitterness and captive to sin." Acts 8:23

I was so enraged by the circumstances surrounding my life! I wanted to hurt the ones who had hurt me. My pain was unbearable. I had anger from childhood inside; I added to that the anger from my broken marriage, and then I was angry with others who had hurt me. I was an angry mess. On top of all of that, I was angry with myself! That's a lot of anger.

I would sit and think about how hurt I was and how I wanted those who had hurt me to experience the consequence of their evil actions. I became very bitter and resentful. I wanted to see justice served. I was leaning on my own understanding, moving in the flesh; hanging on to the poison that unforgiveness will always bring.

I picked up a Kay Arthur book during this time, *When the Hurt Runs Deep*. It was very helpful to me. She talked about the fact that God knows that if anger is not dealt with, it will turn to bitterness quickly and will eat your insides out until you are left a shell of a person. She kept talking, repeating the importance of talking to God about anger, talking to Him out loud. Write it down where you can look at it. Journaling is a good way to see when you began to harbor this malice.

I had so many people telling me to just know that God would not let the ones who had hurt me go unpunished. I would question, but what if God wants me to be the one to stop them. I felt like I was supposed to be Batman or Superman and save the world from these people. I didn't want anyone else to hurt as I was. One pastor would tell me so often, "Tammy, you have to give this to God and trust Him to take care of the ones who have hurt you. He will in His time." He would say, "You may not see what happens, but God will deal with it."

The bitterness and anger had turned to hatred and was eating me alive. I couldn't sleep nor eat. I looked miserable all the time. My mind was constantly running, trying to figure out what to do next. Where was my trust in the Almighty God? Where was the peace that passes all understanding? It was gone for a time. I was not at the point to forgive. I couldn't even consider forgiveness. Yet who was I hurting for all those months? Myself!

Unresolved anger is known to produce some of the following physical, emotional, and spiritual symptoms: (This information comes from J Hunt(2008) Biblical Counseling Keys on Anger: Facing the Fire Within, Dallas, TX: Hope For The Heart.)

Physical Symptoms: High blood pressure, heart disease, stomach disorders, intestinal disorders, headaches, insomnia, compulsive eating

Emotional Symptoms: Anxiety, bitterness, compulsions, depression, fear, insecurity, phobias, worry

Spiritual Symptoms: Loss of Perspective, losing a sense of purpose for your life, loss of sensitivity, becoming a prisoner of your circumstances, loss of confidence, loss of faith, allowing your emotions to distort your thinking, loss of identity, failing to trust God is working in your life, becoming like the person toward whom you are bitter

I know that I had symptoms from each of these lists above. Anger was literally making me sick.

HOLDING ON TO ANGER

I don't know where you are in life or what you are angry about. I do know this. It is hard when you feel betrayed, rejected, abused, unloved, and used. You become angry at God. It happens if we are all honest.

I don't know what kind of fire you are in or how long you have held on to this fury. What I do know is that in order to move on, to ever be whole again, you have to get to the root of the bitterness, and acknowledge what that is, and ask God for the grace to forgive. I had to come to the point to say my anger has turned deadly and is damaging me.

If you are struggling with bitterness then it may be that the Lord is letting the very sin that is flowing from your inability to see Christ be the means by which you come to see Him. In other words, perhaps this season of rage, anger, and fed-up "I'm out of here and don't want anything to do with you" spirit is where you have had to come in order to see the greatness of your sin as a forgiven and justified saint. And the Lord has done it so that you would be stunned at His grace in a deeper way than you've ever been stunned by the grace of God before. And now, out of that experience can flow grace towards others- John Piper

It is only when I came to the place to begin to pour my heart out to God that I felt the anger begin to melt. I had to tell Him everything I was feeling inside. It took a while. It is very hard when you feel so hurt by others. I know! Yet God is waiting for us to do what is right.

THE STORY OF JOSEPH

Think about the story of Joseph in the Bible. His brothers threw him in a pit; then when that wasn't enough, they sold him. What had he done to deserve that? Didn't he have a right to be angry at them? Sure he did. They were jealous of Joseph and his father, so they did away with Joseph. They were tired of Joseph thinking he was better than them. They didn't want to hear about one more dream God had given Joseph. Yet, what does the Bible tell us so clearly Joseph continued to do? It doesn't tell the story of anger and bitterness. It never tells us that Joseph yelled at everyone around him because he was so consumed with wrath against his brothers. It never says that Joseph sat in prison and tried to figure out how to get back at them. I am sure he dealt with being resentful at what his own flesh and blood brothers had done to him. Yet, even after all of this, He did not allow his emotions to rule him.

CHOOSING TO DEAL WITH THE PAIN

It is so hard when the ones we love hurt us. There are no words to describe the pain of being hurt by people we love. Yet Joseph kept on trusting in God. He never let anger take root in his heart. I can imagine that every night he would pray to God and ask God to cleanse Him from any sin he had. In the end Joseph was taken and made second in command in the land. Can you imagine what Joseph was thinking? Joseph trusted God throughout his storm which lasted thirteen years. Thirteen years is a long time. But look what God had waiting for Joseph? Life in the palace.

So what right do I have to harbor a grudge at those who have hurt me so? What right do you have? God has a plan waiting for each one of us after the storm has ended. The same God who had a purpose to Joseph's pain has a purpose for mine.

ASK GOD TO TAKE THE ANGER

I came to the conclusion that God only needs me to pour out all of my feelings to Him. Let Him show me how to deal with the pain. I can't control the actions of others, but I can control my own. I have sat and wondered if the ones who have hurt me so even feel bad? I know the Bible is clear that we will reap what we sow. That is enough for me. The Bible tells me, *"Revenge is mine says the Lord."* (Romans 12:19) He doesn't need my help.

So I have let go of the bitterness that for so long had enslaved my heart. That kind of anger is called sin, my friends. The Bible says, in James, chapter 1: 15 … *that sin when it is full grown, brings forth death.* So let go of your anger. I know how hard it is. There are still days I feel it wanting to rise up, and I have to ask God to please help me. I don't want to live in disobedience do you?

FORGIVING OTHERS AS GOD FORGIVES

I was angry about so many things and at so many people that it took time to work on forgiving others. I found that calling out to God the names of those or whatever had caused my anger was bringing forgiveness to my heart. If your anger is caused by individuals, like me, you will soon begin to feel forgiveness in your heart. You will see the maliciousness dissipate in you. Do it for as long as it takes. Don't stop.

Every day I still pray for these individuals. I sometimes pray that God will make a way to let them know that I forgive them and I am not angry anymore. That may not be part of His plan. The important thing is that I focus on my relationship with Christ. For me to be healthy and whole and fully trusting, I have to let go of anger.

There was a lady who went to church with me. I would observe her as she would come in late and sit on her own. In conversation, she was very short and to the point. She was never involved in any area of the church. She smiled but rarely, and it didn't seem authentic. I could see in her face how anger had taken root and bitterness had set in. I didn't have to know what had happened in her life to cause it; I could see it seeping out of her. I still pray for her when her face comes to my mind. She had a lot of anger inside of her. So what do you think people see when they look at us filled with anger? The same thing! We can act for a while, but eventually it begins to seep throughout our bodies and then people can see it and hear it in us. I have heard the statement many times, "She is going to be a bitter old woman, or he is going to be a bitter old man." What do you think got them there? Unforgiveness!

QUOTING THE SCRIPTURES DAILY

For me it was quoting verses in Psalms that helped me when I was talking to God about all the anger I had in my heart. Psalm 142 really spoke to me one day. The beginning is a cry to God. Does this sound familiar?

This Wasn't Supposed To Be My Life and I Am Angry

I cry out to the Lord with my voice; with my voice to the Lord I make my supplication. I pour out my complaint before Him. I declare before Him my trouble.

David was so overwhelmed with life. He was in a cave talking to God during this Psalm. He was reminding himself in the next few verses that God knew when he was overwhelmed; God knew David's path. Then he tells God that his enemies have set a snare for him; there is no one who acknowledges him. Refuge has failed me; no one cares for me. God please hear my cry. I am so down. Please deliver me from my persecutors because they are stronger than I am. Then David says this, *"Bring my soul out of prison, that I may praise Your name"* (Psalm 142:7).

David felt totally abandoned and alone, and he began to tell God all the things he was feeling in his heart. He was tired of running, and hiding, and wondering when and how he would get out. He was tired of the bitterness that was taking over in his spirit. He wanted deliverance, and he was begging God for it. David asked God to please bring him out of this prison. He couldn't take it. He needed the Lord. He wanted God!

I can totally relate to this Psalm. I was tired of the running that was taking place in my heart and mind. I was tired of the bitterness and unforgiveness that was consuming every vain in my body. I too felt abandoned by God, and so alone. I longed for His presence to fill my heart once again so I begged Him to remove all this dirt from my life. I prayed for God to bring me out of this prison of pain that was causing deterioration in my soul.

Are you tired? Then tell God right now you are letting go of all of these emotions that has engulfed your heart for so long. Even when we don't see it, our anger comes out and affects those around us. Tell God you are laying it down at His feet today. Talk to Him about the bitterness you are carrying around. Don't leave out any details. Then sit back and let Him hold you in His mighty hands. Let Him cradle you and help you get past this pain once and for all. He will do that for you.

Read Psalm 138 now. You can read it all; it is good reading. I am going to jump to verse 8. This excites me for me and for you. Verse 8 says, *The Lord will perfect that which concerns me…. Your mercy endures forever, O Lord, Do NOT forsake the works of Your hands.* Did you hear that, my friends? He is perfecting that which concerns me and you. On top of that, He will never forsake the works of His hands. If you are His child, then that is you! He can handle anything you tell Him about your life. He will help you through your layers of pain, which is the beginning process of healing taking place in you.

Joseph eventually saw his brothers again and told them who he was. Joseph went on to tell his brothers this: *Genesis 50:20, As for you, you meant evil against me; but God mean it for good.* Joseph had begun to heal from the anger and pain of the past. That was evident in this statement. His heart was filled with forgiveness and not anger! That is so wonderful to know, my friends.

IT IS WELL WITH MY SOUL

I love to read the stories of the old hymns, and one story always stays in my mind. There was an attorney in Chicago named Horatio G. Spafford. In 1871 a fire consumed the city and he lost a great amount of money due to his real estate investment. He also lost his only son, who was four years old, to scarlet fever. He decided to take his wife and daughters on a trip to Europe on a much needed vacation. He also wanted to visit D.L . Moody and another evangelist while they were on the trip. Something came up and Spafford had to stay back in New York. He sent his wife and his four daughters on ahead. They were on a beautiful French liner, but Spafford felt a little uneasy about the room they were in, so he had them moved closer to the bow of the ship. He told them good bye and said he would meet them soon. On that voyage their ship collided with an iron sailing vessel, and their ship began to take on water. As much as they all tried to hold on, 226 were swept away into the ocean that day as the ship sank. Horatio's four daughters were among the 226, but his wife was one of 47 who survived. He immediately booked a ship to come and meet her. When his ship came to the spot that was thought to be where his daughters lives were lost, he was called to come out on the deck. After that he couldn't sleep and he penned these words: *When peace like a river attendeth my way, when sorrows like sea billows roll. Whatever my lot, thou hast taught me to say, it is well, it is well, with my soul. It is well, with my soul, it is well, it is well with my soul.*

Horatio Spafford had lost so much; he had every right to be angry. He could have chosen to blame God and the captain of the ship and live the rest of his life as a bitter, angry old man. I can't imagine losing four children; his pain had to be great. Yet during this time, he wrote these great words, a prayer to God. He chose to deal with the pain as it would come in waves and not ignore it. He had such an intimate relationship with God that he told Him about the anger he must have felt and the pain. He didn't let the anger rule his heart. He wrote the last verse about the day he would see the Lord, the same day he would see his children again. Wow! That is my very favorite hymn. Get a copy of that and read the words and let it ring loudly in your heart. He made a choice to live for Christ no matter what. It was well with his soul...

GOD SETS US FREE FROM ANGER AND BITTERNESS

For so long bitterness and anger had me bound. No more! I am redeemed! He set me free! It's so hard when you feel such pain from others. Yet it only hurts us when we dwell on those who have hurt us, so give it up today. It's okay to be angry, but it isn't okay to harbor anger. There are so many days I feel it rise in me, but now I ask God to please take this it away, I don't want it to take root in me anymore. It isn't pretty. Anger looks like a really bad hair day on me. I hate bad hair days, don't you? So let it go.

Do you feel the freedom already? I do. It feels good. I am no longer controlled by the anger that for so long poured through every vein in my body. I gave it to Christ. You do the same right now. Get on your knees and begin to talk to God about your anger. He is always ready to listen and help. After you tell Him, then <u>Be still and listen!</u> He will tell you how to get through wherever you are and how to deal with your angry heart. Do it now! Don't wait another minute!

My sin, oh the bliss of this glorious tho't
My sin not in part But the whole
Is nailed to the cross and I bear it no more, Praise the Lord, Praise the Lord
O my soul.
It is well, with my soul
It is well, it is well, with my soul. (Horatio G. Spafford).

*** Pray * Ponder * Praise ***

Do not merely listen to the word…do what it says. James 1:22

Jesus, for so long anger took residence in my heart. I held on to this anger for so long that bitterness began to take root. Thank You for showing me this had to go because this was sin in my heart. As I pray, search me Oh God and show me anything in me that doesn't please You. You pointed me to this anger that was consuming my life. I thank You for taking the anger away and filling me with more of You. I know that when my heart is filled with other things it quickly fills Your place. I do not want the sin of anger clinging so close to my heart. I am saddened of the thought of this anger being where Your spirit lives inside of me. Thank You for Your Holy Spirit convicting my heart and penetrating my soul. My heart is Your home, only You. I don't want other things to take up residence inside of me that begin to choke out Your spirit, where others can't see you but the anger. Thank You for showing me my sin. It's so easy to see the sins of others, but that is not my place to be their judge. It is my place to deal with my heart. Lord, I ask You for more of You, flood my soul with more of You. You are my redeemer. Your mercies are new every morning. I want others to see Your love and joy in my heart, not anger. Thank You, Jesus, for Your love and for removing the anger that once held on to my heart. In Your sweet name I pray, Amen.

- Are you holding on to anger in your heart?
- Can you go back to the exact time this bitterness began to take root?
- Are you ready to surrender your anger to God?
- Who are you hurting by holding on to anger inside of you?

Sometimes we hold on to anger because we are so mad at someone else. Yet, the anger is hurting us, not them. Get your paper out and write down why you are angry and who you are angry with. Now go to God in prayer with this paper. Read it to Jesus. He already knows, but it will help you to tell Him out loud. Now throw that paper away!

Psalm 139:23, *Search me, O God, and know my heart; try me, and know my anxieties.*

Psalm 145:8, *The Lord is gracious and full of compassion, slow to anger and great in mercy.*

Ephesians 4:31, *Let all bitterness, wrath, anger; clamor, and evil speaking by put away from you, with all malice. And be kind one to another, tenderhearted, forgiving one another, even as God in Christ forgave you.*

Sweet hour of prayer, sweet hour of prayer
That calls me from a world of care,
and bids me at my Father's throne, make all my wants and wishes known
In seasons of distress and grief, my soul has often found relief
And oft escaped the tempter's snare, by Thy return, sweet hour of prayer
(William W. Walford and William B. Bradbury)

CHAPTER 6

Satan's Attacks On Christian Lives

When I read the story I just wrote down for you, I am still amazed that this is my story. That is what happened to my life. Not long ago I was so excited at how God was using me in ministry. I could see God was doing a work in my life. Beware, however, because that is when satan is ready to attack. So I want to warn you as Christians to be ready.

WHO SATAN REALLY IS

The Bible tells us in I Peter 5:8, *Be alert and sober minded. Your enemy the devil prowls around like a roaring lion looking for someone to devour.* We must guard our minds and our hearts against satan's attacks. I thought I was guarding my mind and soul but he knew where to attack me.

Satan doesn't want our lives to be used for kingdom purposes. He wants to destroy any chance we have to influence this world for Christ. The biggest way he can do that is by our testimony. I was teaching the women in my church and enjoying the Bible studies I was leading, and satan knew he had to find a way to stop the work of Christ. It is always his primary goal. I know that I wasn't spending as much time in prayer as I had in the past. When we stop praying, trouble is on the way.

Thus Far

The one concern of the devil is to keep Christians from praying. He fears nothing from prayerless studies, prayerless work, and prayerless religion. He laughs at our toil, mocks at our wisdom, but trembles when we pray –
Samuel Chadwick

Years of being in an extremely dysfunctional marriage left me vulnerable and open to the seduction of the devil. The enemy of my soul knew just what I needed to hear to cause me to let my guard down a little at a time, and I totally fell into his trap. Everything I loved—from God's Word, to worship, to deep emotional talks were part of the very seductions the enemy used to hook me. It was like I was being groomed by a predator. Satan used God's very Word to draw me into a relationship that he knew would destroy lives. That was his plan. He was waiting to wage warfare on my life! I had longed since I was a child just to be loved and satan used this to draw me into his clutches a little at a time. He saw where I was weak and he came to sift me.

Choices that I made led to a chain of events that caused devastation in many lives. Don't kid yourself that our sin doesn't affect those around us. *Sin will always affect those around us whether we see the immediate connection or not. I'm sure Achan thought his sin would go unnoticed and not impact anyone else…but thirty-six innocent men died and fear came upon an entire nation! Never think that your sin or my sin is a personal matter. God has related us together and our sin affects others.* (free-bible-study-lessons.com)

The other person's sin affected me and in turn my sin affected others. Satan was thrilled. His plan had worked. At least that is what he thought.

For me, even after time had passed and I was really trying to live for Christ, satan would continue to attack my mind. If he can get into our minds, he has us.

WHEN SATAN ATTACKS THE MIND

As my transgressions became common knowledge, I began to experience despair, depression, and undescriable panic; everything I had been trying to hide was coming to the surface. As a way of coping, I began to run. I have never run in my entire life nor ever wanted to. But I would run for miles. I cannot tell you how many times I stopped along the side of the road convulsing with sobs and paralyzed with grief. My mind kept replaying the past and it would cause me to focus on all I had lost again and again. I was being sucked into a continual vortex of sorrow, shame and condemnation.

I began to fervently pray as I walked and asked God to guard my mind and help me to take those thoughts captive. II Corinthians 10:5 speaks to this very thing. Let's go back to verse 4, which says, *For the weapons of our warfare are not carnal but mighty in God for pulling down strongholds, casting down arguments and every high thing that exalts itself against the knowledge of God, bringing every thought into captivity to the obedience of Christ.* So whenever my mind wanted to go back I would say verses or ask God to fill my mind with more of Him. He arms us with the sword, the Word of God, to stand against the enemy's lies. Isaiah 54:17 tells us, *No weapon formed against you will prosper...* 2 Thess. 3:3, *But the Lord is faithful, and He will strengthen you and protect you from the evil one.* Luke 10:19, *Behold, I have given you authority to tread on serpents and scorpions, and over all the power of the enemy, and nothing shall hurt you.* John 10:10, *The thief comes only to steal and kill and destroy. I come that they may have life and have it abundantly.* This is how you fight against the devil, by quoting the word of God.

For so many years I had been angry with my husband for the pornography he looked at, and I couldn't understand why he couldn't just quit. Finally I understood. Once you allow satan in and he has an area that he knows is your weakness, he will attack every opportunity he can. He used what I had just lived through to attack my mind over and over. This way he kept me bound.

The Bible talks so much about guarding our hearts and minds. Proverbs 4:23, *Keep your heart with all diligence, for out of it springs the issues of life.*

None of us is exempt from being tempted. It's how we handle the temptation that matters. I wasn't guarding my heart. We must be diligent to guard our hearts because our heart is extremely valuable. . Michael Hyatt says this, *It is the essence of who you are. It is where all your dreams, desires, and passions live. It is the part of you that connects with God and other people. Solomon is saying, above all else, in other words, make it your top priority to guard it. The second reason is because your heart is the source of everything you do. King Solomon says it is the "wellspring of life." In other words, it's the source of everything else in your life. Your heart overflows into thoughts, words, and actions. The third reason is because your heart is under constant attack. He implies when King Solomon says guard your heart, that you are living in a combat zone—one which there are casualties. We have an enemy who is bent on our destruction. He not only opposes God, but he opposes everything that is aligned with Him- including us.*

As women we all seek to be loved and listened to and appreciated. I had not felt that for so long. I really didn't think it mattered so much to me. I wasn't following the guidelines above for guarding my heart. I was in the combat zone, and allowing satan to batter my heart over and over. It was painful.

Ravi Zacharias had this to say about the heart:

If you look at the book of Proverbs you'll find the word "heart" again and again. Solomon talked about the heart because he lost his heart to many women. But he reminds us, "My son, give me your heart" (Proverbs 23:26). This is because your entire spiritual journey and the threads that God wants to pull together will be determined by who owns your heart. (The Grand Weaver: How God Shapes Us Through the Events of Our Lives, Ravi Zacharias)

God is the only one who can bring our hearts and minds into submission to Him. But I was still enjoying thinking back—it was an issue of my heart. I loved to think about *his* touch, about the time we spent praying together, talking, laughing, just enjoying each other's company. It was difficult for me to stop thinking about *him*. So satan would keep attacking me as long as I was giving in; satan was waging war against my heart and soul.

Satan WAGES WAR AGAINST CHRISTIANS

If you had asked me, before my fall, I would have said that I would never fall into temptation. I read God's Word, and I would not let the adversary into my life. Yet I did. Never say never!! He wages war against Christians daily and he will not stop! Satan wants to find any way he can to keep the gospel from being spread. At the point in my life where God was using me to influence women, satan saw this as an opportunity to ruin my testimony for Christ, and lessen my godly impact on those around me.

2 Corinthians 4: 4 says, *Whose minds the god of this age has blinded, who do not believe, lest the light of the gospel of the glory of Christ, should shine on them.* I was so bound in sin and blinded to it for a time. If satan can keep us blinded, he can keep us bound. I was reading the Bible but reliving the past daily in my mind. I began to fight hard in my mind and write Bible verses on cards and try to memorize them. You can fight the attacks if you want to badly enough. I decided satan would not have my life.

BOUND BY FEAR

Another way satan tries to bind us is by fear. I will be honest. I fight fears many days. I was very depressed for a time. I would stay home because my fear of facing people was so great. Because I was a public person in my community, and had lived there my entire life, it seemed my life was public knowledge. I felt judged by so many; I hated the way they looked at me in public. I felt dirty and condemned by these individuals. I shopped at different grocery stores; I totally rearranged my life because I feared seeing people. Sounds crazy now, but fear consumed me. Once I got past that fear,

I was left with the fear of being on my own for the first time. I had been married since I was nineteen and had never had the sole responsibility of taking care of my needs. I was terrified. There are many days that fear takes over and I sit and try to figure it all out again. That is satan. I don't have to figure it out. God is going to take care of me. Satan is the author of fear and doubt. This is a hard one because even the strongest Christian has to deal with fear at some point.

The definition of fear is *an unpleasant emotion caused by the belief that someone or something is dangerous, likely to cause pain, or a threat* (Oxford Dictionary). Have you ever had something that you were very fearful of? Is there something that causes you to tremble at the very sight of it?

MY FEAR OF SNAKES

I am terrified of snakes. Honestly, I am so terrified that I can't even look at one on the television. In all reality, I haven't seen one up close in several years. Sounds crazy, huh? But I pray every time I walk down the road, that God won't let me see a snake. So far, so good!

It's wonderful to climb the liquid mountains of the sky. Behind me and before me is God and I have no fears- Helen Keller

So why do we let fear drive us into a corner? We know God is greater than any fear, right? Then we need to remember that. II Timothy 1:7 tells us, *For God has not given us a spirit of fear, but power and of love and of a sound mind.* We don't need to live in fear about the future. God is already there. We can't let fear control us. I may not ever see a snake up close, so I need to know that I can't walk around waiting for it to bite me. How crazy would that be? You would call me a psycho if I told you I am not going out because there might be a snake on the road. You would think I had lost my mind. Yet we choose to be a slave to fear because of something that might happen. That is a lack of trust. We need to know we serve a mighty God who is ready to handle every fear we have. I am speaking to myself in that. So don't let satan keep you bound in fear. I John 4:18 says, *There is no fear in love. But perfect love drives out fear, because fear has to do with punishment. The one who fears is not made perfect in love.* No one is perfect and God knows this, which is why He sprinkled encouragement against fear all through the Bible. He keeps reminding us, "Fear Not." He tells us not to be afraid of being alone, of being too weak, of not being heard, and of lacking physical needs. Psalm 56:11 reminds us, *In God I trust; I will not be afraid. What can man do to me?* Choose today to say the scripture over and over if you have to, but don't let fear grip your soul. Know it is an attack from satan. Anything he can do he will to keep reminding us of everything we fear.

It is by putting on the whole armor of God that we are free from the power of satan in this world. Ephesians 6:10-18 says, *Finally, my brethren, be strong in the Lord and in the power of His might. Put on the whole armor of God, that you may be able to stand against the wiles of the devil. For we do not wrestle against flesh and blood, but against principalities, against powers, against the rulers of the darkness of this age, against spiritual hosts of wickedness in the heavenly places. Therefore take up the whole armor of God, that you may be able to withstand in the evil day, and having done all, to stand. Stand therefore, having girded your waist with truth, having put on the breastplate of righteousness, and having shod your feet with the preparation of the gospel of peace; above all, taking the shield of faith with which you will be able to quench all the fiery darts of the wicked one. And take the helmet of salvation, and the sword of the Spirit, which is the word of God; praying always with all prayer and supplication in the Spirit, being watchful to this end with all perseverance and supplication for all the saints.*

So we need six things to be ready for warfare:

Belt of truth, breastplate of righteousness, shoes of peace, shield of faith, helmet of salvation, and sword of the Spirit.

Pastor, speaker, and author, Tony Evans says: *"The first three pieces of the armor begins with the word 'having', taken from the verb 'to be.' This means that the first three pieces of armor are pieces that you should wear all of the time. You should never take them off. They are like a uniform a baseball player puts on when he goes onto the field. The last three pieces of the armor are given to you to pick up as the situation demands. We are told to "take" them up. This is like that same baseball player either grabbing his glove or his bat, depending on what is going on in the game. God has, through the armor, supplied everything you and I need to live a life of complete victory in spiritual warfare. It is our job, through faith, to use each piece of what He has given us. God is not going to dress us, but He has given us what we need to be armed for victory. It's time to suit up and be well-dressed for warfare."* (The Urban Alternative Christian Daily Radio Broadcast, Tony Evans)

God pulled me from the horrible pit as found in Psalms, and I am so thankful. My eyes are focused on Christ. I have on my armor, prepared for the battle. I must be on guard and hiding God's Word in my heart daily to fight off the works of satan. He is alive and real in this world. He wants to destroy any effort for God's Word to be shared with this world. We must determine not to give in to fleshly desires. I realize even as I write this that the prince of darkness is waiting for the chance to try to stop me from opening my mouth and sharing my story. He wants to tell me I am not good enough. I am not worthy for Christ to use me. That is a lie from the devil. God is a God of second chances. Do I hear an amen? God is a God of second chances. I am so thankful for that. I will not let satan deceive me into thinking I am not worthy to spread the gospel. I am determined to hide God's Word in my heart and be ready for these attacks when they come. The old hymn says, "Satan had me bound but Jesus lifted me" (Evelyn Simpson-Curenton arr). I love that line. Keep a song in your heart today and a verse ready at all times. Fight, my friends. God created us to spread His Word and He never promised it would be easy.

Look at the story of our Savior. He experienced fear, just as we have.

Jesus didn't want to suffer. He asked His Father to let the cup pass from Him. He knew the cruel death He was about to face. But it was God's will for Jesus to die on the cross. Without Jesus' suffering we would not know the victory of the resurrection! He broke the power of my sin with His death on the cross. Fear had no hold on Him! He trusted God's plan and was obedient, even to death. Jesus willingly died for you and me. That is the greatest story in history. So get up today and work for Him, the one who created you. The one who did not let fear have a hold but choose rather to suffer to bring us victory!

Whatever you are going through, ask God to be with you through the fire. How I love Isaiah 43, *When you pass through the waters, I will be with you; and through the rivers, they shall not overflow you. When you walk through the fire, you shall not be burned, Nor shall the flames scorch you. For I am the Lord Your God.* That is shouting scripture. I love it. I read that over and over some days. You can do it. Get up. God will give you the strength. Don't let satan keep you down. I wasted precious time I could have been working for Christ. There is a lost and dying world that needs us to spread the word of salvation. The people need our stories and our hope. Will you let satan win and keep you bound? Or will you fight and give your worries to Christ and let Him fight for you?

Let these words strengthen you today. Deuteronomy 33:26-27, *"There is no one like the God of Jeshurun, who rides the heavens to help you, and in His excellency on the clouds. The eternal God is your refuge, and underneath are the everlasting arms; He will thrust out the enemy from before you, and will say, Destroy!"* !" That is our God, the one true God. You can trust Him to deliver you today. My friend just reminded me of a song that says, "There is no God like Jehovah, there is no God like Jehovah" (Robin Mark). How exciting is that. It is true; there is no God like Jehovah!

I am well aware today that satan is waiting to attack me again. But I am ready. Are you? A.W. Tozier had this to say: **"The only safe place for a sheep is by his Shepherd. Because the devil does not fear sheep, he only fears**

the Shepherd." So the more time I spend with Jesus in His Word and in prayer, the closer I become to Him. This is a sure way to keep satan away! Walk close to our Great Shepherd, Jesus Christ!

I must daily hide His Word in my heart and throughout the day talk to God. I must always be armed for battle, by having the armor of God in place in my life. I put on praise music when I am in the car. There is a song that says, "The chains that seem to bind you, drop powerless behind you, when you praise Him." So today give satan a good swift kick and say, as my dad would say, "Get behind me satan."

Do not merely listen to the word...do what it says. James 1:22

Jesus, I know that I left a door open for satan to come in. He is waiting to seek whom he may devour. I am sorry that I was really arrogant and thought satan wouldn't get me. He had been looking for a way to destroy me for my whole life. He found a way in. I know he will continue to attack my life. Jesus, I am trusting You and looking to You daily to fight for me. The battle is Yours! In the name of Jesus I tell satan to get away from my life; he has no place here. I am a child of God, a daughter of the King of all Kings, He is my Lord, not you satan. So get away from me and my family. God, help me to hide Your word in my heart daily to ward off the attacks of the devil. I know he will not leave us alone. His plan is to destroy my life, but Your plan is to give me life and to give it more abundantly. You are my strength and my fortress, You are my God. Help me to keep my eyes on You and not on the things of this world. Help me not to be enticed by the desires of the flesh, but to look to You to fill the desires of my life. I command, satan to get away. He has no place in my life or the lives of my family. You have authority over me, and only You. You broke the power of canceled sin, You set the prisoner free, You are the one and only God. You rule my heart and life. Thank You for Your mercies that are new every day. I know when I walk through the waters they will not overflow me, and I will not be burned in the desert because You, my God, are with me wherever I go, guiding me, protecting me. You are my shield, my help in times of trouble. I call on Your name, and my enemy is placed under Your feet. You are for me! If God be for me, who can be against me? I am Yours, Lord. Take my life and use it for Your glory. Thank you for reminding me that every battle is Yours, not mine. I need only stand still; You will fight for me. The battle is already won in You, Christ Jesus, my Lord. It's in Your powerful name I pray, thanking You for going before in the battles yet to come. I love You Lord. In Your sweet name I pray. Amen and Amen!

- How is satan attacking you right now in your life?
- What are you doing to stay grounded in Christ?
- Is there a small opening in your life that satan is waiting to walk through?
- If so, what is it and what can you do today to prevent this attack?

Go back and remember the battles satan has waged on your life. Now remember they are in your past and God fought for you. Name some of these battles that you have won already.

Satan is like a roaring lion, seeking whom he may devour. So keep yourself planted in God's Word and never forget the promises God has given us. Greater is He that is within me, than he that is in this world. God wins every time! You must be ready; so keep yourself in the faith, ready at all times. He will attack; you must get on your knees and ask God to fight the battle. It is here battles are won!

Teach my song to rise to You, when temptation comes my way
When I cannot stand I'll fall on You
Jesus, You're my hope and stay
Lord I need You, Oh, I need You
Every hour I need You
My one defense, my righteousness
Oh, God how I need You
(Daniel Carson, Matt Maher, Jesse Reeves, Kristian Stanfill, Christy Nockels)

CHAPTER 7

Strongholds

I have heard about strongholds for so long. What is a stronghold, you might be asking? I read in Beth Moore's book, *Praying God's Word*, that it is anything that exalts itself in our minds, "pretending" to be bigger or more powerful than our God. It might be alcohol, drugs, despair, unforgiveness, whatever it is it consumes our mind most of the time. I have watched people who couldn't give up alcohol before. It broke my heart as I watched their lives crumble. One of my dear friends has a brother who is addicted to drugs. I have watched over and over as he has made horrible mistakes because of the stronghold these drugs have on him. It was heartbreaking to watch these individuals crumble because satan had strongholds on their lives.

It's funny as I type this and listen to myself, now I can see how my friends felt watching me. I thought I was so strong, that nothing could ever have a hold on me. I watched my husband and the devastation to his life because of the stronghold of pornography. I would just wonder why he couldn't walk away from it. I didn't understand the hold it had on him. He would often say, "I wanted to get caught; I so wanted out." You could see the death grip it had on him. I would just get angry and think it was crazy because he wouldn't give it up.

Who would have thought I would have a stronghold. Not me! I am the last person. I would have argued with you and sworn that it would never happen to me. I was still bound by the emotional affair. I still wanted all the communication, my mind was very bound. I tried to get out of where I was; but it had such a hold on me, I didn't know how to get out. It felt good. I went by how it felt.

BLIND AND BOUND

During this time a friend asked me to do a video Bible study with her. I really didn't want to but I knew she wanted to help me so I went. She had asked me to choose one, I chose *Breaking Free by Beth Moore*. I was amazed by how this video spoke to my very situation. Isn't it great when God does that for us? But I was bound. I thought, "How can I do this?" satan for a time had me blinded that it wasn't a stronghold, just a friendship. What was wrong with that? But I knew. I would cry at night but longed for the connection every day. The hold satan had on me was strong, and I couldn't see it for so long.

A soul tie to anyone besides our spouse is outside the will of God and becomes an open target for the continuing, destroying schemes of the devil-
Beth Moore
(Praying God's Word)

There is no happiness when you are bound to sin. I had a sin issue, bottom line. Call it what you want to. I know the word sin is not popular in this day. But it was sin in my life. Until I could see the sin, my friends could talk until they were blue in the face and it didn't change anything.

DAVID HAD A STRONGHOLD

When David saw Bathsheba on the rooftop, he had her brought to him. We have all heard this story. She was beautiful and in his mind the fact that she was married wasn't bothering him at the time. He just knew he wanted her. Her husband was in David's army so he was fighting a war. It seemed perfect. They could enjoy their time together and her hubby would never know. Oops! Wrong! Bathsheba ended up pregnant. Can you imagine the devastation David had when she told him this news? Now how was he going to hide? He had a plan. He would bring Uriah, her husband, home, and he could sleep with Bathsheba. A perfect plan. Then no one would know the baby was David's. But Uriah wouldn't do that. He knew that during a battle he was to refrain from sexual activity as a soldier. He was loyal to that. So David had a problem! He decided to have Uriah killed quickly. I would say if you put someone on the front line in a battle they are pretty much going down. So that is what he did. He had Joab put Uriah on the frontline. He was killed, then David could take Bathsheba and no one would know. When we lie the first time, there is always more that follow to cover the first one! So he was lying to cover himself. That is how deceived he was. He didn't see his own state. Satan had him bound. All he knew was that he wanted Bathsheba. That was the important thing to him at the time.

LIVING IN THE MOMENT

When we have a stronghold in our life, we want what we want, and that is all that matters. It's in the front of our mind all the time. When we lie the first time, the second lie is always easier. So David just kept going. He was doing what I was doing—living in the moment. It felt good. She was beautiful and he was the king. I told my friends many times to quit worrying, that I was in control. Even though this was an emotional affair and not a sexual affair like David was in, I thought I could handle it. I am sure the devil was in the corner laughing and saying that he would show me as he watched his plan unfold!

A STRONGHOLD IS SIN

2 Samuel 11:27 says, *David took Bathsheba for his wife after the mourning over her husband ceased; she became his wife and bore him a son. But the thing that David had done displeased the Lord.* We can't cover sin and think we are going to prosper. It doesn't matter who we are—David, the King, the friend of God, or the man on the street. **Sin is sin.** A stronghold is sin! I didn't see this stronghold. I was bound and deceived by the author of deceit himself. How did I ever think that I could prosper when it was so outside of God's will? Yet, I did. I was enjoying this; yet to my friends, I looked miserable. They would ask me what was going on, and I would lie and say nothing. I had one sweet friend begging me to please walk away. I never admitted to her that anything was going on, but she knew. She would beg and plead with me that I was going to get hurt, or caught, but I cared about him at this point and I didn't want God's ways if it meant giving him up. So I would just say what everyone wanted to hear and never tell them what was really going on. On one hand I knew I was wrong but I was happy. I look back now and think, "Tammy, where were you?" Yet the Bible says there is pleasure in sin for a season. I was ignoring the voice of God over and over, telling me to flee!

As I shared earlier, satan had me bound in my mind. Yet through a chain of events, God got my attention. He has a way of doing that. He breaks us down until all we have is Him. He wouldn't have to go so far, but sometimes it takes something devastating to get our attention.

After the emotional relationship ended, I then thought finding a man was the answer to everything. I was divorced now. But as the song says, I was looking for love in all the wrong places. Still not ready to surrender to the Lord. At the time I was in a dating relationship I had no business in, it led to me losing my job, and not knowing how I would survive. But it was at the bottom of the pit I began crying out to God and telling Him I knew I needed to turn from the sin that had me bound. I begged Him to take this stronghold away. I got out my Bible and started writing verses on index cards and reading them aloud each day. This is how I broke through the stronghold. God's Word is sharper than a two-edged sword the Bible says. Let's read the verse together. Hebrews 4:12 *For the Word of God is living and powerful, and sharper than any two-edged sword, piercing even to the division of soul and spirit, and of joints and marrow, and is a discerner of the thoughts and intents of the heart.* I began to get on my face and cry out to God with these verses. Now I was waging battle against the schemes of the devil. I was telling him I was going to break down this hold he had on me. I was going to live victoriously. I was going to get up and make my life count for Christ. So I made it a point to begin each day by setting aside time for God in the mornings. It felt so good to feel God moving in my heart. I felt chains of anger falling and chains of bitterness falling. I felt forgiveness in my heart. The enemy was trembling now. I still had a long way to go. Yet I felt more peace than I can begin to tell you. I didn't care if I had to eat ramen noodles; I was so happy to feel restored. There is a song that says, "In prisoners chains with bleeding hearts, Paul and Silas prayed that night. And IN their pain began to sing, their chains were loosed and they were free" (Marcus Hummon, Bobby Boyd, Jeff Hanna). That is how I felt. Relief flooded my soul. It was evident to all who saw me that my chains had fallen off, and I was free.

PLACING THE STRONGHOLD UNDER HIS FEET

I know I have to keep myself in the Word because satan is going to fight. I remember the Breaking Free Bible study (Beth Moore) one night talking about strongholds and temptations. I wrote in the margin of my book what my temptation was. Under it I wrote, hard-hardest-easier-UNDER HIS FEET. When I began to hate the sin, the stronghold, and cry out to God and beg him to take it, He did. Now it is under His feet. Jesus delivered me!

I was thinking about this one day. How can I truly place this under His feet, never to be picked up again? Because if you are like me I have a tendency to want to give it to God but then I began to slowly take it back. I have never done this, but I have always wanted to slam a plate on the floor. Just throw it and watch it shatter into a million pieces. Seems like a good stress reliever! So what if we thought about our temptations and strongholds like this. We have a glass plate that represents whatever we need to hand to Jesus, whatever is holding us captive. So we hand this plate to Jesus and He takes it and places it under His feet and stomps on it. It shreds into a million pieces. He looks at us and says "Now I have taken your burden and you will never have to pick it up again, it is under my feet, forever." Jesus looks up and says, "you will never carry this burden again, you are free!" Isn't that a blessed picture? Jesus does what we couldn't do for ourselves. John 8:32 reminds me, *You shall know the truth, and the truth shall make you free.*

I don't know where you are in your battle. But I want you to get out your Bible and quote the verses within its pages. Get on your face and beg God to show you where to study in His Word. Fight the power of satan. God is stronger! I would open the book I referred to earlier, *Praying God's Word* and just read it aloud. There is something about reading scripture out loud. Maybe I think satan will hear me the louder I read and he will run away! I don't know, but I like to read out loud when I am home.

GOD BREAKS THE STRONGHOLDS

James 1:14 tells us *that each one is tempted when he is drawn away by his own desires and enticed. Then when desire has conceived, it gives birth to sin; and sin, when it is full-grown, brings forth death.* God knew we would be tempted by the desires of this world. That's why we have to fight so hard and have His Word engrained in us to break these strongholds. We have to want to change. There are many days I say these verses aloud. I want to live in obedience and I want satan to hear me quote God's Word and get away from me. Finally I was ready to let go. God knew all those other times I was still holding on to sin. Now I was ready to move on.

Strongholds

I want to give you seven ways to disarm strongholds of the mind (by Rebecca Greenwood)

1. By receiving the Father's Love.
2. By identifying sin, repenting and changing. We have to lay down the old self, strip off the sinful nature, disarm sinful desires and embrace Christlikeness.
3. Being filled with His Spirit
4. Living a Life of Forgiveness
5. Staying in the Word
6. Worship God! Spend time with Him
7. Don't entertain lies. We must choose not to listen when the enemy attempts to invade our thoughts and speak lies. Choose to refuse him entrance!

So give your battle to God and He will fight, fight, fight the battle for you. Place your stronghold under His feet and let Him show you the way. Say the verses aloud. You will experience victory! That is where I am. I am watching Him restore me and confirm me. He loves me so much. I love this verse I Peter 5:10, *After you have suffered a while, our God, who is full of kindness through Christ, will give you His eternal glory. He personally will come and pick you up, and set you firmly in place, and make you stronger than ever.* I love it. I could stand and shout. That verse is powerful. I know my heavenly Father hated to watch me jumping off the same cliff over and over again. It was agonizing for Him because He loves me more than anyone ever could. When I came before Him and asked Him to deliver me from the bondage of sin, He did! He then picked me up and held me in His strong and mighty arms, and He gave me His strength. Without Him I am nothing, but with Christ I have everything I need to face the battle! Praise God through Him I have won, I have won, sin is defeated!

During this season of life, I had a good friend call me. She said, "Today, let this be the day you stop. Erase the number and let us surround you and help you have an accountability group." They so wanted to see me free. But I wasn't ready. So I kept on going in my sin. Oh if I could go back, let pride go, and have heeded her advice. It would have saved me so much suffering. So today, lay it down at the feet of Jesus. Break free today. Get on your knees and beg God to help you, plunge into His everlasting arms. He is all we need. He is waiting for you to see this. Christ is enough.

Jesus You're all that I need, Jesus You're all that I need
When I think I'm alone in this valley, I feel Your arms 'round me.
In Your haven I will stay Lord, I will rest and wait for thee
For it's here, I am learning, Jesus You're all I need (Tammy Daniel).

*** Pray * Ponder * Praise ***

Do not merely listen to the word…do what it says. James 1:22

Jesus, I thank You for breaking the stronghold in my life. God, for so long I walked around holding on and not willing to even admit I had a stronghold. Thank You for loving me so much that daily You began to penetrate my heart with Your Holy Spirit to show me that I was the only one who could come to You and then You could break the power this stronghold had on me. For so long I was bound and felt hopeless. I just couldn't let go. I held on because I wanted my fleshly desires to be filled. I was wrong Lord. I know it's only through Your power that I am free today from the stronghold in my life. You delivered me from the battle. You showed me that with You there is life, only with You. You showed me that when I am weak then You are made strong. You broke the chains and set this prisoner free. Thank you Jesus! You are my healer and my redeemer! You are fighting for me, pushing back the powers of darkness right now. It is only in You I can say this stronghold will no longer bind me! I am no longer bound in these chains. You commanded satan to break the chains and they were broken in Your name. Jesus, I beg You for whoever is struggling right now with a stronghold of their lives that they fall on their knees and beg You for mercy and grace and only then will they feel the chains that bind them fall to the ground. In Your name they will find healing. So I beg You for those reading this that Your spirit would speak to them and they would stop wherever they are and command the chains to fall off. Thank You Jesus for deliverance in my own life. I bless Your name for You are the Life, the Truth, and the Way. Deliverance will only come when we bow to You and ask You to break the power this sin has on us. Thank You for victory that You have given me over sin. May I keep my eyes focused on You and only You. Thank You for being my King. I love You, Lord. In your powerful name I pray. Amen!

- What stronghold do you have in your life or have you experienced in the past?
- What is keeping you from letting go?
- Do you believe that God can break the power this stronghold has on you or your loved one?

Get on your knees wherever you are and in the name of Jesus command satan to let go of you. If you are a child of God, ask God to loose the chains, and they will fall. If you have never asked Jesus into Your life, then stop right now and ask him to come into Your heart and be ruler of Your life. Ask Him to forgive You of the sin in Your life. He loves you and He wants You to experience the freedom of a life in Christ. He came to bind the brokenhearted and set the captives free. He will set you free, if you will ask Him today. Let go of the stronghold today. Now, you may need to seek the help of a friend, counselor, or minister to give you some guidance. Have a friend you trust to hold you accountable. Do you want to live in victory today? Then take the steps to do that. I am praying for you! This is a big day; you can do this with Your hand in Jesus' hand. Let Him set you free once and for all!

In the dark of the midnight, Have I oft hid my face
While the storms howl above me, and there's no hiding place
Mid the crash of the thunder, Precious Lord hear my cry
Keep my safe 'til the storm passes by
Till the storm passes over,' till the thunder sounds no more
Till the clouds roll forever from the sky
Hold me fast, let me stand in the hollow of Thy hand
Keep my safe, till the storm passes by (Mosie Lister)

CHAPTER 8

Getting Through The Storm

So now I had determined to once again live for Christ. The storm was still raging but I was letting the Master of the Sea be my guide. Although I was a Bible teacher to women and had faith and joy, my faith had never been put to the test like this. I had a hard time with God. Why did I need to go through this to begin with? Yet God had not put me through anything; I had made the choices.

HOW CAN ANY OF THIS BE FOR GOOD

Yet before I ever fell, He knew this would happen. I know "all things work together for good", but what good could there possibly be in this storm? So some years back, I was deep in depression as I stated earlier, not weathering the storm very well. The faith I had shared my entire life was not seen right then. I let shame and anger and regret take over. I was not getting through the storm well. I felt as though this would be my defining moment. For the rest of my life it would be how I was viewed. I let the storm define me. How do you get through something that is so devastating? You might be trying to get through the loss of a loved one, or finding out you have cancer, or losing your job, or going through a divorce. Whatever it is, how do we get through the storm?

I went to a wonderful ladies' conference recently. It was a joy to be there. My pastor's wife was speaking and I couldn't wait to hear what she had to say. There was wonderful music, and oh how I loved once again praising my Lord. For me music is how I release some of my stress. During much of my depression and the time I was bound, I didn't play the piano. My song seemed to be gone. But at the conference I loved the beautiful music. I heard others speak openly about depression and how it had them down. I heard my friend speak of her cancer that she had been through and many other things. Yet in the midst of it, she spoke about God making something beautiful of these storms in our lives. She quoted this old song: "Something beautiful, something good, all my confusion He understood. All I had to offer Him was brokenness and strife, and He made something beautiful of my life" (Bill Gaither). I sat there with tears streaming down my face. I had felt so confused for so long. But the song says, He understood. I tried for so long to get through this on my own. I had tried to hurt the other people who had hurt me. That only led to more pain for me. The song goes on to say, "All I had to offer Him was brokenness and strife." That was all I had. I was so broken I didn't think God could fix me. It felt too big. How could God possibly make good out of this storm? But the song says, "He made something beautiful of my life." God wants us to lean on Him to get through the storm. He is our strength. The Bible tells us in Luke 1:37, *For with God nothing will be impossible.* If God didn't mean that He wouldn't have put it in His Word. He means it. My storm seemed hopeless, but it wasn't. I had to realize that to get through the storm all I had to do was lean on His everlasting arms. He would do the rest. At the conference that weekend I heard another woman speak on getting through her storm. It resounded in my mind and heart. I felt alive and hopeful.

I CAN'T GET THROUGH THE STORM

Today you may be saying like me, "I can't get through this." You can. Get up out of bed. I remember lying on my couch one night in total darkness for hours. A friend drove by my house and saw my car, so she called because there were no lights on. She said, "Get up and turn the lights on." I said, "I will in a bit." I hung up and lay there not wanting to live. She called back and said, "Get up and turn the lights on." That day was dark, and I didn't want to get up. I wanted to close my eyes and never wake up. So I know how you feel. But get up today and turn the lights on. Get up and go walk. Just get up. Today you have to start to determine that you will make it through your storm.

ELISABETH ELLIOT

I read about a missionary by the name of Elisabeth Elliot. She indeed knows about getting through a rough storm. She and her husband Jim Elliot went to serve in the jungles of Ecuador. She and the other missionary wives received word one day that two bodies had been found at the location where their husbands had gone. Can you imagine what was going through her mind as she wondered if one of those bodies belonged to her husband?

Yet the first thing she did was focus her mind on God and the truth in His Word. "A verse God had impressed on my mind when I first arrived in Ecuador came back suddenly and sharply: When thou passes through the waters, I will be with thee, and through the rivers, they shall not overflow thee…"She then prayed and she says, "I went upstairs to continue teaching the Indian girls' literacy class, praying silently, Lord, let not the waters overflow." (Elisabeth Elliot, *Through Gates of Splendor*)

Jim Elliot was one of the men who was killed. Can you imagine the crisis Elisabeth faced in a foreign land? Yet she exhibited faith in Christ through this horrific death. When she didn't want to press on to get through this storm, this is what she did: "At such times I have been wonderfully calmed and strengthened by doing some simple duty…like a bed to be made or a kitchen floor to be washed…sometimes it takes everything you have to get up and do it, but it is surprising how strength comes." She continues, "There is wonderful therapy in getting up and doing something. While you are doing, time passes quickly. Time itself will in some measure heal…And in the doing of whatever comes next, we are shown what to do after that."

How did she remain calm and determine to make is through this storm? She had an intimate relationship with Jesus. She says, "Our Lord did not halt all activity to brood over what was to come, He was not incapacitated by the fear of suffering, though He knew that fear. To the question, 'What shall I do?' he simply answered, 'This,' and did what lay in His path to do at the moment, trusting himself completely into the hands of His Father. This is how He endured the cross." (Elisabeth Elliot, *Twelve Baskets of Crumbs*, Elizabeth George, *Loving God with All Your Mind*)

Mrs. Elliot lived her life and was able to make it through this storm because she was surrendered to God. This is where I was on my journey, a place of surrender, full surrender to God.

SWEET SURRENDER

When I came to the place that I could see Christ was all I needed, I began to see Him at work. I was looking for a job and it seemed every job I applied for fell through. It seemed every door I opened slammed shut in my face. I began to cry out to God and say, "Okay, Lord, I am depending on you. I don't know what you have for me, but I cannot get through this without you." That was all He needed to hear. A friend had given me a paper sometime back with verses and different biblical quotes to help me draw nearer to Christ. I want to quote to you one of those nuggets: "You know you're surrendered to God when you rely on God to work things out instead of trying to manipulate others, force your agenda, and control the situation. You don't always have to be 'in charge.' Surrender doesn't weaken you; it strengthens you." Whoa! That statement hit me right between the eyes. Here I was once again trying to control this situation. It was at that moment God said to me, "You know how you're going to get through this storm, by totally surrendering everything to me. " I smiled that day as I sat on my couch. I began to pray and tell God to take my life, all of it. I was His. Take my anger, my bitterness, unforgiveness, all of me and make me what He desired me to be. My friends, when we totally surrender to God we can get through any storm. Any storm! Did you hear me? How are you and I going to weather the storm we are in: by totally, fully surrendering to God.

How many times have we sung the invitation hymn, "I surrender all, I surrender all, all to thee my blessed Savior, I surrender all" (Judson W Van DeVenter). SURRENDER is the key to everything.

God's peace flooded my soul that day. I began to feel restoration coming. The battle was still raging, but I knew God had complete control. I began to immediately see God at work. I teach piano lessons but didn't have enough students to survive. Before I could even advertise for more lessons, three people called me to sign their children up. Then another called, and when I advertised on my Facebook page, three more students signed up. God was supplying my every need as only He could.

I was standing in my living room talking to the mom of one of my piano students, when I heard God say, "Tell her you need a job." I just kept on talking to her, and I heard His voice again say, "Tell her you need a job." So I figured out how to work into the conversation that I was looking for a part-time job. She looked at me and said, "My boss told me yesterday to look for someone to work part-time with us; she will hire you, I am sure." I was so excited! She did hire me and it has been the perfect job! I got on my knees and praised Him for this job!

For a little while, He opened a door for me to sing in a southern gospel singing group and travel some on weekends. I still didn't have quite what I need to live, but I had no doubt God was going to provide. He was taking me through the storm. The song the group gave me to sing was the old hymn,

"Till the Storm Passes by" (Mosie Lister). I was able to give a testimony, sharing how God had brought me through some raging waters. I was so thankful God allowed me to encourage a weary soul that day. I could speak with great confidence of how I could not have made it through without Jesus.

If the Lord had not been on our side...the raging waters would have swept us away...Psalm 124:2-4

I know I still have much to face but not alone. God is with me, carrying me even when I can't walk. I don't know where you are in your storm, but I want you to know you will get through. Get your Bible out daily and read, even if it's one verse. All day quote that verse. Each day tell God you are surrendering this storm to Him. Be honest with God. He knows us better than anyone, He is our best friend. Talk to Him like you would your girlfriend or your mom, or whomever you share your life with. Take your burden to the Lord and leave it there, the old hymn says. He wants to carry your heavy load. He is capable of taking care of you. It struck me when I was able to go to this ladies' conference that if He could provide a way for me to get to enjoy a weekend that wasn't a necessity, He was capable of providing my every need.

IT TAKES PATIENCE TO GET THROUGH

I tell everyone that I am not a very patient person. My dear friends will tell you this is so true. So like you, I want to get through this storm quickly and get to whatever God has waiting on the other side. The truth is I don't know what is waiting on the other side. I have no idea how quickly God is going to choose to reveal that to me. My job is to sit and wait. He will take me through to the other side in His way and in His time. That is hard, isn't it? I just want God to heal me now. I want to wake up in the morning and be the winner of the Publishers Clearing House one million dollars.

But the reality is that probably isn't going to happen. It would be nice if it did, but I don't think so. James tells us in chapter 5 and verse 10 that the prophets who spoke in the name of the Lord are an example of suffering and patience. He went on to say we count them blessed who endure. You have heard of the perseverance of Job. God placed all of these real people in the Bible as examples for us to make it through the storm. Job stayed true to God. Look at all he lost but still he remained faithful. There are so many verses in the Bible about waiting. *"Wait on the Lord and be of good courage and He shall strengthen your heart; wait I say on the Lord"* (Psalm 27:14). So it takes patience to make it through the storm.

So, number one to get through the storm is surrendering to God. Then we must be patient. Only then will we endure and see the other side of the storm. Psalm 30 says, *Weeping may endure for the night but joy comes in the morning.* It may seem your tears are endless, but it will seem just a short time until you can look back and smile again. If we want the crown God has waiting for us, we must endure to get through the storm.

PRAISING HIM IN THE STORM

I love the story of Paul and Silas in prison. It was not a good experience to be in prison in those days. It was a cold dark prison that I picture in my mind. They were chained up for teaching the gospel. They could have chosen to be angry and scream at God. Yet in the midnight hour they were singing praises to their King, I love it. The Bible says in Acts Chapter 8 that the other prisoners were listening to them. Oh my, people are watching and listening to us during our storms. This was very convicting for me to ponder; I didn't like the way I had handled myself during this season of my life. I was determined to exemplify God's grace moving forward.

There was an earthquake in the prison and their chains fell off. They could have run out of the prison, which is what I would have done. Yet they patiently waited. The guard was going to kill himself because the soldiers would kill him anyway for the prisoners leaving that he was supposed to be guarding. Paul and Silas told him they weren't fleeing the scene, and he was startled. They took this opportunity to share Jesus with this guard. Because of this, he asked them how to be saved. He wanted what they had. That day, the Bible tells us, he and his entire household came to know Christ, all because Paul and Silas allowed God to use them in the storm. Wow!

So how can we get through the storm? Be determined to praise Him in the storm! Our joy is not dependent upon our circumstances but on our God. Listen to the song that says, *I will praise You in the storm, I will lift my hands....* (Bernie Herms, Mark Hall) Get your CD player out, or your phone, your MP3, whatever you can listen to praise music on. Try it, and you will be amazed at how much better you will feel. There are times I find myself falling on my knees and lifting my hands to heaven as I lift my voice in praise. I like to turn my music on in the kitchen really loudly and sing along. I have my own concert right there at the kitchen sink. I love how worship music takes me from where I am and places me at the feet of Jesus, in His very presence. Put in a CD and let the lyrics fill your heart; now you can begin to praise Him to get through the storm.

God opened a door for me to be able to sing again. I felt God had opened the door because the timing was perfect. So I didn't hesitate to walk through. Yet I still was questioning God as to why this group? A few weeks into it we were headed to a photo shoot. One of the ladies was beside me; none of us knew each other very well. So I was just making small talk. I asked her where she attended church. She looked puzzled. She began to share that she had just changed churches because of her marriage. She said, "I have been married 17 years and our marriage is in trouble. We have attended the same church for years where we have been living a lie." She continued, "My husband is a deacon and a Sunday school teacher. He teaches about marriage, yet ours is awful. I have asked him for us to seek help from the church, but he refuses to. He doesn't see the problem." She said, "In church he will put his arm around me and pretend all is well with us." She said, "I can't do it anymore. It is wrong to live a lie. So I left the church and went to another." My mouth could have dropped open as she went on. I knew why God had placed me in this group; it was to minister to this lady. She had such a sweet spirit and desired to do the right thing in the sight of God. That day I just listened to her and told her I would pray for her situation. When I left that night, all I could think of was that I had to share my life with her. I know God has placed me here to witness to her and encourage her. So two weeks later when the time was right, I shared my story with her. We sat in a hotel room with tears streaming as I told her I knew exactly how she felt. We both knew that God had placed us together. I felt like my pain suddenly had a purpose. I was able to encourage a dear sister whom God had placed in my path. I felt God telling me, "Tammy, open your mouth and be transparent; a whole world of people needs to be encouraged that they too can get through the storm."

PERSEVERANCE

One realization I had to come to and confess was that I had created part of the storm. It is true. I made some choices that I will have to live with forever that only made my life harder. I read this morning that when God puts a road block in front of us, we shouldn't go plowing through or try to figure out a way to get through it; we need to understand He has it blocked for a reason.

If we go driving down the interstate and suddenly see a sign which says, "left lane closed ahead", then we have to get into the other lane. If we don't, we will have to sit and wait. We have to do what the sign says. We aren't allowed to drive through the cones. If we decide to drive through the cones it will not be good. We have to follow the signs that have been placed there to protect us from injury. That's what God does for us. He closes and blocks some paths because we do not need to even consider going that way. I know that I blew right through the signs and made my storm much worse in the end. So we have to listen when God says, "I don't want you to go that way." It is our job as believers to obey and know He knows the path in which we should walk. Yet the wonderful thing about our loving God is that even when we break down the barriers and plow through the road block, He forgives us and helps us find our way back. Proverbs 4:26-27: *Ponder the path of your feet, and let all your ways be established. Do not turn to the right or to the left; remove your foot from evil.* This verse reminds us how important it is to focus on the path God has for us and not to look away. It only makes it harder to get through the storm when we resist the path that leads to Godliness. So to get through the storm, persevere, and don't get off the path God has chosen for you. Even though it seems bumpy, ride it out.

GOD IS MOLDING YOU IN THE STORM

We must believe God has a reason for the storm we are in. It's been so hard for me to see the reason in my life. I have questioned God so many times. There are some questions we will never have answers for until we get to heaven. We just have to fix our eyes on Him for He knows what He has waiting for us. Today I can look at a woman and say I know how it feels to be used by a man. I know how it feels to want to die. I know how it feels to feel shame when you walk in a store and feel the whole town is judging you. I know how it feels to be rejected. I know how it feels to hear your husband say that he doesn't want to work it out but wants a divorce. I know how it feels to worry how you will provide for yourself and your children. I know how it feels to have your heart so broken you think it will never mend. Now I can pray with someone and truly feel their pain.

I read today, *Iron till it be thoroughly heated is incapable to be wrought, so God sees good to cast some into the furnace of affliction, and then beats them on His anvil into what frame He pleases (Anne Bradstreet)* I feel like I have been beaten really well. The truth is I need to smile, knowing my God loves me so much, He is beating me and making me into the person He desires.

God has a plan far greater than anything I could imagine; He is working for my good and yours even when we cannot see it. So may we weather the storm because He is beating out the bad and filling us with more of Him, making us more like Him. God in all of His providence and omnipotence is the skillful artist and our lives are His tapestry which sometimes helps to make sense of the insensible.

> *Life is But A Weaving (The Tapestry Poem)*
> *My life is but a weaving between my God and me.*
> *I cannot choose the colors He weaveth steadily.*
>
> *Oft' times He weaveth sorrow; And I in foolish pride*
> *Forget He sees the upper and I the underside.*
>
> *Not 'til the loom is silent and the shuttles cease to fly*
> *Will God unroll the canvas and reveal the reasons why.*
>
> *The dark threads are as needful in the weaver's skillful hand.*
> *As the threads of gold and silver in the pattern He has planned.*
>
> *He knows, He loves, He cares; Nothing this truth can dim.*
> *He gives the very best to those who leave the choice to Him - Corrie Ten Boom*

So how will we get through the storm? We do this by surrendering to Him, by being patient, by not pushing through the road blocks, and by praising Him. He is weaving our lives into a beautiful tapestry as only He can weave. We will sit back in the years to come and all we will see is the beautiful picture He has made of our lives. I don't know when the end will come, but I am now going to walk through the rest of this storm hand in hand with my Jesus.

Psalm 23: "The Lord is my Shepherd": that's relationship. "I shall not want": that's supply. "He makes me to lie down in green pastures": that's rest. "He leads me beside still waters": that's refreshment. "He restores my soul": that's healing. "He leads me in the paths of righteousness": that's guidance. "For His name's sake": that's purpose. "Yea though I walk through the valley of the shadow of death": that's testing. "I will fear no evil": that's protection. "For you are with me": that's faithfulness. "Your rod and your staff, they comfort me": that's discipline. "You prepare a table for me in the presence of my enemies": that's hope. "You anoint my head with oil": that's consecration. "My cup overflows": that's abundance." Surely goodness and mercy shall follow me all the days of my life": that's blessing. "And I will dwell in the house of the Lord" that's security. "Forever": that's eternity. (Author Unknown)

Your disappointments do matter because the Shepherd of your soul will put it all together for you and has an eternity for you to revel in the marvel of what God has done. Our Father holds the threads of the design, and I'm so immensely grateful that He is the Grand Weaver. (Ravi Zacharias)

You know by now that I have a song for everything. Google the song, "The Anchor Holds" by Ray Boltz. I love the words to this song. May the words encourage your heart today! Surrender fully to God and wait; our great Shepherd, the Grand Weaver will carry you through the storm, my friends!

I have journeyed though the long dark night
Out on the open sea; by faith alone, sight unknown
Yet His eyes were watching me.
The Anchor Holds, though the ship is battered; the anchor holds, though the
sails are torn.
I have fallen on my knees, as I face the raging seas,
But the anchor holds, in spite of the storm.
I've had visions, and I've had dreams; I've even held them in my hands

Getting Through The Storm

I never knew, they could slip right through, like they were only grains of
sand.
But the anchor holds, though the ship is battered; the anchor holds, though
the sails are torn.
I have fallen on my knees, as I've face the raging seas,
But the anchor holds, in spite of the storm.
I have been young, but I'm older now
There has been beauty, these eyes have seen;
But it was in the night, in the storm of my life
That's where God proved His love for me.
And the anchor holds, though the ships been battered; the anchor holds,
though the sails are torn
I have fallen on my knees, as I faced the raging seas, the anchor holds, in
spite of the storm (Ray Boltz)

*** Pray * Ponder * Praise ***

Do not merely listen to the word...do what it says. James 1:22

Jesus, I thank You for showing me that You were carrying me through the storm. You amaze me that You love me and want to help me through the storm even though I created some of this mess. You love me despite the big mess I made. I thank You for hiding me in the crevice of the rock until I was ready to fly again. You are my strength. When I was overwhelmed You knew my way and You came to me. You are my rock, Jesus. I could not have made it through this storm without You. You comfort me and make me to lie down in green pastures, You lead me beside the still waters. You quiet my soul. You showed me that my joy was not dependent upon my circumstances but was in You. I have sweet joy in my soul that only You can give. With You holding me up I can walk through any storm that comes my way. You want to lead me through the valley to the mountain. You showed me that all I needed was Your hand in mine. You covered me with Your love and grace. You carried me until I could walk again. You gave me hope when I felt hopeless. You gave me peace in the midst of the battle. You know I am not a very patient person and I hate waiting. You taught me that I have to wait on Your timing and learn to be patient. I praise You for walking with me and holding my hand. I praise You for You alone deserve my praise. I praise You for drawing me out of deep waters. I praise You for showing me that all things do work together for good to those who love You. I praise You because You are my God and worthy of all praise. Nothing shall separate me from Your love, not distress, not tribulation, not persecution. I am so thankful that You taught me I had to surrender all to You, and You were enough to carry me through the storm. I love You Jesus. Thank You for loving me and saving me. It's in Your great name I pray. Amen

- What storm are you facing today?
- Describe a time when Christ carried you through the storm.
- What did He teach you in this storm?
- Was there a time you felt you could not get through the storm?
- What happened to make you determined you would get through the storm?

You may be facing sickness today, divorce, financial troubles, issues with your children, addictions. I don't know where you are. I do know Christ wants to carry you through the storm. Stop and ask Him to help you; He is all You need to get through whatever has come your way. Trust Him to know it will take time to get through the storm, but He has a perfect plan. So rest in Him today. He will carry you when you are too weak to walk. He has promised in His word never to forsake you or leave you alone. Determine today to praise Him either way. He is worthy of your praise.

Habakkuk 3:17-18, *Though the fig tree may not blossom, nor fruit be on the vines; though the labor of the olive may fail, and the fields yield no food; (though I have cancer, divorce, a sick child, financial issues, etc.) though the flock may be cut off from the fold, and there be no herd in the stalls- Yet I will rejoice in the Lord; I will joy in the God of my salvation.*
Psalm 57:1
Psalm 27:14

I know you're somewhere on your knees
Somewhere the Father stops to hear you intercede
You had me on your mind, and you took the time to pray for me
Somewhere on your knees (Joel Lindsey and Janet Paschal)

CHAPTER 9

Weathering the Storm Together

I love my friends. My goodness, God has blessed me with friends during every season of my life. I am smiling, thinking back through the years at the fun I have had with my friends. I dearly love them.

I will never forget a statement I heard during a message that has stayed with me. We don't need any fair weather friends. I wrote that down in my Bible and pondered over that. I didn't know at that time I would watch that statement become very real in my life. I believe it, don't you? I want friends in my life who not only have fun with me but are willing to walk with me through anything that comes my way. I know God sometimes weeds out for us the relationships we don't need and replaces them with lifelong friendships.

FRIENDSHIP

For such a time as this, God has blessed me with some wonderful dear sisters in Christ. This group has weathered many difficult times with me. I want to tell you that each one of them would like to have strangled me along the way, but I am still alive and kicking. Thankfully, they didn't kill me! They wanted to strongly shake me in Jesus' name a few times, I know that. I put them all through so much, but they have been so faithful to me. I am honored that God has placed each one of these dear ladies in my life. As I look back I can see just what an awesome God we serve, a God who sent total strangers my way whom I learned to love dearly.

Right before I began heavy warfare, God placed one of these strangers in my life that He knew I would need. I was teaching a Bible study in the lower income housing community once a week. I loved it. These ladies were hungry for God's Word. After a women's meeting at church, Judy ask me if she could begin coming with me. I said sure. I was glad someone else was interested in loving on these women who so desperately needed to hear about and see the love of God. What I didn't know how God was about to use this stranger not only in these ladies' lives but in mine as well. We went each week for months, sharing God's Word and a meal with these ladies. I saw how much effort she put into the food she brought. It was great. Slowly I was learning about my new friend and enjoying her. Every week when I would prepare the lesson to teach these ladies, it was about storms and second chances. It was where I was. Judy began to teach; she was an excellent communicator. God's love easily flowed out of her to all of us in the room.

One night she came up and talked to me about Bible study the next night. I couldn't hear her for the turmoil going on in my mind. I don't know if you have ever been so upset that your mind was running in circles, but that is where I was that night. I was sitting in my seat but my mind was a million miles away. She sensed this and texted me later. She said, "I don't know what is wrong but I am praying for you." I still didn't tell her. She never pressured me to tell her what was wrong. She never asked. At one point I felt I should share with her a small portion of what I had been dealing with. I knew I needed to take a break from the Bible study I was teaching because my heart was not in it. She thanked me for telling her and said she would pray.

Time passed and I really never expected to hear from her. Then she came to me and told me that God had placed me on her heart. She said that she was going to spend every Wednesday night with me. We could walk, have dinner or have Bible study. But she felt God had told her to use this time to minister to me. God was looking out for me. Some weeks we would go out and eat or she would cook for me. My appetite wasn't great at the time. Sometimes we would go to town and walk. We would talk about my marriage and she would share with me about her life, using her story to help me through mine. Some nights we would do Bible study. She was so patient with me, meeting me where I was. Isn't that what ministry is? Finding a need and meeting it and finding a hurting and healing it. She is now one of my dearest friends.

She would beg me to break free and watch me fighting it. She would watch me start to move back closer to God but then flesh would take over again. When the emotional affair ended I couldn't eat or sleep for weeks. The very first night as I lay in my bed trying to relax, I was talking to her on the phone. I was telling her my body felt like it was crawling and I couldn't take it. She prayed and tried to help calm me so I could relax and sleep. She told me how hard it was to watch me jump off the same cliff over and over. Yet she never left my side, just kept praying and reaching out to me. I love her so much. She is a jewel that God has given me. I am so thankful for this friendship. Had it not been for her many days of calling and just letting me know that she cared I would have given up a long time ago. See how much God loves us? He took someone who was a stranger and made her a lifelong friend. She encourages me all the time that God has a plan to use me to minister. She will never know how much she means to me. The time she has given has made a difference for eternity.

FRIENDS STAND WITH YOU IN THE STORMS

Then there are several others who have always stood by me. A dear friend of mine gave me money when I desperately needed it. I will never forget that. I know she didn't have it, yet she gave it. Another precious friend watched me continue to disobey God, yet still she stood by me. I know it genuinely concerned her. She had gone through the loss of her brother and I know her heart was so heavy, yet she listened to me. She would read me passages from books and beg me to be the one to stop. I know she was praying also. She was crying out to God on my behalf. She never left my side. We still continue to laugh together and cry together some days. I know she is happy we are laughing some now.

A few of my lifelong friends would check on me and walk with me. They would let me talk. It didn't matter what I said; they would listen. I needed to talk about what I had been through. I needed to talk about it and grieve the loss. They didn't tell me how crazy I was; they cried with me. I know they didn't always want to hear what I had to say, but they listened and were just there. That is all I needed. Some days I would cry for what seemed like hours, and one of them would hold me or listen. They didn't judge me at all; they loved me regardless. They all gave me such a wonderful support system.

I must tell you about my dear Priscilla. She has been so good to me. Some weeks we talk every morning. She allows me to say what I need to say, and know that she will always listen and never walk away. She knows me probably better than anyone at this point in my life. There have been days I haven't liked what she had to say to me, but I needed to hear it. There are days I would get angry with her, but I knew down deep inside she was right, so after a few days, I would call her back to talk it out with her. She gave me the security in my life that I needed. She has helped me face many hard days, always pointing me to Jesus. I love her dearly, and am blessed to have her.

Where one would leave off, the other would just take up. I know it was hard for them to see where I was. They were so used to me wanting to go to lunch or have a party. Now I only wanted to stay at home, alone. If I did go out, I couldn't wait to get back home. I felt secure at home. That was hard for them. I was nothing like the woman I had been months before. At one point I know they wondered if I would ever come out on the other side of my isolation. Just recently they shared with me that they didn't think

I was going to make it at one point. They watched me suffer from severe depression, then they were there as bitterness was setting it, I know that was so hard for them. I had some very dark days. Yet they each had a part in my healing. They did whatever it took each week to help me. What a blessing each one was to me! They became my support system, my accountability, my everything. Faithful friends! I pray God blesses their lives for the faithfulness they have shown me.

On my birthday I really didn't feel like celebrating, yet three wonderful ladies took me to lunch. We had such a good time. We laughed and ate together. I will never forget it. I needed to laugh. One sweet friend went to pray over our lunch and, because of something comical that was said before she began to pray, she laughed through the whole prayer. It was hilarious. Every time she regained her voice she would burst into laughter again. Then we would all join in. I had tears streaming down my face after the prayer from laughing so hard. I know God has a great sense of humor and He understood. She refuses to pray out loud anymore when we are together in a restaurant. That makes me laugh even more. That was a great day and I will never forget the laughter that took place at that table. I love those ladies. They are dear friends to me.

WHAT JESUS SAYS ABOUT FRIENDSHIP

Isn't that the kind of friend Jesus tells us to be? They are true examples of what a friend is. A friend, the Bible says, loves at all times (Proverbs 17:17). All times means loving someone even when you don't agree with them. Now each one of these ladies was quick to tell me they didn't like what I was saying and doing; I knew that, yet they didn't let that keep them from loving me. I had deceived them so badly, but they loved me still. I felt so bad knowing that this trial had been so hard on so many. I felt the weight of this continually, but at the time I didn't have much to give.

Emotionally, physically, and spiritually, I was drained. So I was dependent upon them. A little too dependent at times, I know that now. I know some of them are saying a little dependent? Excuse me. **Very dependent**. I was very afraid of losing someone else, so I held on tightly to these women. This is still a great battle for me at times. I fear losing them so much at times that they have to make me release the death grip I have on them. But finally they can see my dependence on Christ and not so much on them.

I am so thankful for each one of them and how they let God use them during this time. They truly kept me from going over the edge. One friend kept inviting me to where she was attending church. It seemed a little ways for me to drive but she was insistent that I would love it. I finally went and she was right; I loved it. I know God placed me there to help me heal. I so appreciate her keeping on with me until I finally went. She has become one of my dearest friends in this storm. I love my church and am so thankful God has planted me there for such a time as this. She will never know how God has used her during these dark days to lift me up. She listened countless hours as I would break down over the phone, she would listen and encourage me in the Word of God.

What I am trying to tell you is that I love these women and they weathered the greatest storm I have ever been through with me. That is what friends do. Now in this season of life God is sending new friends my way. I am stronger now and I am able to put something into a friendship. For so long I truly had nothing to give. Just last weekend God placed in my path two ladies I attend church with that I didn't know. I am so thankful for these new friendships. Possibly I will be able to weather a storm with them.

If you were my friend one thing you would know about me is I love to laugh, and I love to be with people. I am all about game night and just going out with girlfriends every now and then. I had a group of girlfriends and every Christmas we would go out and shop until we dropped. We would plan this trip for weeks. We would start talking about it in the summer. One day of no children and eating wherever and however many times we wanted to. It was great.

HURT PEOPLE, HURT PEOPLE

I had several friends I had hurt during this time and I wanted to fix those friendships, but with my counselor urged me to work on ME during this time and not try to mend fences. My healing had to come first in order for me to be able to have anything to give in a friendship. I trust a great big God who can restore and heal these friendships if that is part of His plan. If not, I am so content with my life and the ones He has placed in it. They are perfect! Why should that surprise me? I serve a God who loves me so much that He gave me these friends. Let me tell you I am probably going to mess up again if Jesus doesn't come back soon. We all mess up. I need friends who aren't expecting perfection but will love me just the same. I love that these girls can hang with me. I feel like God just handpicked them and placed them in my life for such a time as this.

I was having coffee a few months back with a new sweet friend of mine. She was talking about a friend who was going through a hard time. She asked me what she could do for this friend. Like my friends, she wanted to shake her friend and make her see what she was doing. I told her the best thing she could do was just be there. Even when her friend made choices she didn't agree with, she should just listen and let her know she was there. That is tough to do. I feel so bad now that I can look back on what my friends have endured. It is hard to watch someone you love make mistake after mistake and not listen to reason. I know it grieved their hearts to watch me suffer. But they let me come to the place to let Christ open my eyes. I couldn't wait to call each one of them when He began restoring me.

GOD GIVES US FRIENDS FOR ALL SEASONS

I have to tell you about one in particular. I received an email from a lady I didn't know very well. This email said that I might think she was crazy but she felt like God had placed me on her mind. She went on to say she wanted to be a friend. She felt that God had wanted her to pray for me daily. She said she gets goose bumps when she called my name to God. I read this email and had to stop driving. What was God up to? I called her that afternoon. I didn't know why God had placed me on her mind, but I wanted to talk to her. I went to her and we prayed together. She told me she felt like God wanted to use my life if I could just get to the top of the mountain to see what He had waiting on the other side. I sat and listened. It was just a short time after meeting with her I went into my deep depression and life fell apart. Months after that she contacted me. She said she didn't need to hear what I had been through; she didn't care. She still prayed for me and believed God wanted to use my life. She is one of the people who pushed me to write this book. I thank God He placed her in my life. I know she prays for me and I love her. So now God has placed two strangers in my life and used them to keep my eyes pointed to Him. Who can do that but our wonderful Lord, the King of Kings, the one and only true God.

JESUS LOVED HIS FRIEND LAZARUS

Friends are such a gift in this life. It reminds me of Lazarus. He was Jesus' friend, the brother of Mary and Martha. Lazarus became sick and died. They called for Jesus to come. Jesus didn't come right away. The ladies were so sad. Their brother had died and they kept thinking that if only Jesus had come He could have healed him. They thought He was their brother's friend; but if He were where was He? Jesus tarried where He was. It wasn't until four days later that he came. They greeted Jesus and said if He had been there He could have healed Lazarus and he would still be alive but Jesus hadn't come. I love this story for many reasons. Jesus did love Lazarus. You know Jesus could have chosen to have healed him from afar or bring him back to life from afar. Jesus didn't have to come to where they were. Yet He chose to come to Mary and Martha. You see, Jesus loved Lazarus and He hated how much they were hurting. He knew He could heal Lazarus. Yet our Lord wanted to come and cry with these ladies. I love this picture. Jesus wanted to feel what we feel, so He came and sat and cried with them over the loss of their brother. After that Jesus chose to raise Lazarus from the dead. Everyone there was able to witness the glory of the Lord! I am sure at that point Mary and Martha were so happy and yet they had doubted our Lord. This is a story of friendship. I am sure this story spread like a wild fire that He had raised Lazarus from the dead. He didn't just heal him He gave him life again. Wow! What a picture of friendship!

WE ALL NEED FRIENDS

I don't know where you are in life, but we all need friends. Remember the old Proverb: *"To be a friend, you must first show yourself friendly"* (Proverb 18:24). So if you have no friends maybe you need to take a look at why. That is hard. I know that I was not the friend I should have been a while back. Friends are God's gifts to us here on earth. We need each other. I want to be able to be myself with my friends. No walls, just enjoying life together. I learned that life is too short to worry about the little things. I am me, and little old me is not always good. So I am glad these girls have learned that and still wanted to stick around. Sometimes we have to work at being a good friend. There are many times I have to apologize for being quick to say something I shouldn't or expecting too much.

One of my dear older friends gave me two devotional books that I love. When I read them I think of her. She will never know how much Jesus has spoken to me through these two books. One is a *Jesus Calling* devotional book and it seems daily God just speaks to me through the words on that page. Like me, you probably see a gift from a friend, and it reminds you of them; and hopefully, it brings a smile to your face. I think of her and pray for her many days when I pick up these devotionals.

I have a beautiful happy box that a friend gave me for Christmas. I fill it with things that have made me happy so that on the bad days I can open it and remember and smile. I love this box, my happy box! I recently found an

8 x 10 photo of one of my friends and me. I was wearing "Bubba teeth." You know those if you live in Tennessee. They look like a mouth full of rotten teeth or buck teeth. I guess some people think that's what we look like here in Tennessee. I should never have worn those in the picture; I should have known it would come back to me. Sure enough, it came in the mail, blown up as the 8x10; and it was hilarious. I had to laugh when I looked at the picture. Crazy friends! It's in my happy box!

So wherever you are in life, thank God for your friends. Let them know that you love them and appreciate them. Go out and have fun together and laugh.

PRAYING WITH FRIENDS

When I felt the calling on my life, I decided to call all of my friends that had stood with me through the fire and ask them to meet me to pray. Now I know they will probably bring all kinds of oil to pour on me and pray that I never mess up so badly again!! I cannot describe to you in words how God was in that room with us that Sunday afternoon. I wanted them all in a room for two reasons. I wanted them to meet each other. Not everyone knew the other ones. It was fun to watch them meet. It felt like a reunion in a sense. We went inside the church auditorium and sat in a circle. One friend didn't know anyone else. She was the stranger God had asked to pray for me all that time long ago. So I went around the room and told her about each lady sitting there. I felt tears come to my eyes as I shared what they each had done for me over the past two years. Then I told them about Maggie, the stranger only one of the ladies knew. Maggie spoke about the day God had asked her to pray for me. It was great to hear her tell this story. I just sat in awe that God loved me that much, hearing it again. I then told the ladies I was sorry for what I had put them through. It was a day of releasing the past to move on. They all told me they had no hard feelings. Then each began to share their concerns for me as I moved on to the calling

I felt God had on my life. They all had the same message. Be patient and wait on God. They have gotten to know me well; they know I am not good at waiting! I expressed that I wanted them to be my accountability group. If I were having a weak thought then I would tell one of them at least. I ask them to tell me if they saw anything in me that was not pleasing to Christ. I expressed that I truly wanted to go forward and please my God. As we sat in a circle and held hands, we prayed. We had a "Come to Jesus hallelujah revival." God's presence was over us in that room. It was amazing. Then I played the piano and sang: "I've wandered far away from God, but now I'm coming home. The paths of sin too long I've trod, Now I'm coming home… (William J. Kirkpatrick) I wanted them to see and hear what God had done for me. It was a great afternoon. Jesus met with us and the past was the past. I don't have to wonder if they are praying for me. I know they are. It goes both ways!

I am laughing, thinking of each one of them as I type. I want to be the kind of friend that will laugh with you and pray with you and hold you during the bad times. My friends are great. There's one who always tells me when my hair needs to get the gray out! I love it. I love gray, but I am not ready for it yet. So she helps me with my hair. We all know if our hair is bad, then it is a bad day. So I am thankful for her.

It's really funny as I think on this group of ladies God has blessed me with; they are all pretty spotless. I am not sure what God is telling me. I am not spotless; I have never been. My house is clean but not clutter free. It is funny to me as I think on all of their homes and the clutter free atmosphere. I was laughing with a friend this morning, telling her about this. Since I first wrote this, I went back in my mind to each one of their homes; and I am telling you, they are all so spotless and have no clutter in the corners. I met a new friend from where I go to church, and she is a professional organizer! God is really trying to tell me something.

One time the burglar alarm went off at my home. I had just had my second baby and was nursing for the first time. It was a pretty rough few days. My downstairs was clean but upstairs had stuff everywhere. I was rearranging the boy's rooms and had clothes everywhere. My room was just a disaster with drawers open and clothes all over the place. I hope I can blame this on depression after the baby came. Sounds good anyway. Well my mom wanted me to bring the new baby to her hair dresser's home. After I left, my alarm went off. I went racing home to find three patrol cars in my driveway. The Sheriff, a tall man, put his arm around me and said, "Ma'am, I don't want to alarm you; but we think your house has been ransacked!!!" I could have laughed out loud. I prayed that as I went through the door that someone had been in there and ransacked it, but I had a bad feeling. He told me to go in and see if everything was the way I had left it. I went upstairs and wanted to come screaming down and say, "No, someone has been here;" but I couldn't lie. So I came down, and never looked him in the eye and said, "Yes, Sir, everything is the way I left it." I wanted to crawl under a rock. LOL. I do have better order than that now, I want you to know. Nonetheless, my friends love that story. It has never happened to any of them in their clutter free, spotless environment. Oh well, they have boring stories to tell!! I hope you are laughing; go ahead, it was funny. I made the mistake of telling one friend and the story spread like a wild fire. I love to be in a crowd and hear one of these dear, sweet friends say, "Tammy, tell them that story about your house!" The look on my face would be, I will kill you after we leave here. I got used to it and learned to laugh at myself. These are my friends. Clutter-free friends!

YOU DON'T HAVE TO WEATHER THE STORMS ALONE

So, the point of this chapter is that I don't want to weather a storm alone. I was reading in Proverbs about being a friend. This is what my Bible says: Long term friendship is precious indeed. We cannot choose brothers or sisters; but a friend, freely chosen, can sometimes be closer than a *blood* relative. Often a relative lives far away, and a friend who is nearby is an immediate help in time of trial. Galatians 6:2 talks about bearing one another's burdens. We need each other. Proverbs 27:17 talks about iron sharpening iron, so a man sharpens the countenance of his friend. I want this kind of friends. I value every person that has been a friend to me.

A GREAT CHRISTIAN COUNSELOR

My counselor would tell me how important it was that I be able to share what I was feeling with at least one friend. It was so true. I needed to talk about what I had been through. It was all part of the healing process. As my counselor would share with me she would say it isn't going to happen fast. She was so right. As I talked to her, I felt as though I could give my friends an emotional break too. Yet they were so kind to say they were fine. I knew they were tired too. The journey had been long and I was exhausted emotionally, spiritually, and physically, and they were also.

My counselor is great and helped me know that I wasn't crazy because of the pain I was feeling. I sometimes would cry for the entire hour I was with her. I was working through an enormous amount of emotional baggage. Sometimes I would cry over my marriage, and talk about the years of unhappiness I had faced. Other times I would talk of the pain the emotional affair had caused my heart and the shame and regrets I was living with. I would leave her office exhausted from the excruciating sobs from the present situation and just talking through all the years of tormenting pain in my past. We talked through how to find peace in Christ and His love, and how I was searching in the wrong places seeking love.

I am so happy that I sought and got help. It's okay to talk to someone when life comes at you hard. So I would like to encourage you never to hesitate seeking good Godly counseling when you are in a battle. She helped me see the light at the end of the tunnel, and she allowed me to cry and cry and cry. It felt really good to be able to let it all out so that healing could take place. Although I was sharing with friends, they weren't trained to help me with healing and processing all that I had been through. My counselor was. So don't think you are weak if you need counseling. I am truly so thankful for the friend who cared enough to tell me to call a counselor and the church which paid for me to go. She helped me focus on what was important at that time to help me heal and move forward. There were books she had me purchase to help me with my pain. One was a book called *Boundaries* by Dr. Henry Cloud and Dr. John Townsend. It was great. It took me a while to be able to concentrate enough to read it. So I encourage you to take advantage of a good counselor.

Weathering the storm… we need each other. My friends and I have truly been on a long journey through a long, dark storm. I am so thankful they weathered it with me. They will never know how God used their words, their smiles, their laughter, their tears, and their arms of love. They are such examples to me of being a good friend. I was talking to one of them recently about my heart's desire which is to speak to women about my painful past and to be transparent. She said she couldn't wait to sit and hear me speak and watch God use me. What a friend!!! I love her so much. I know they wanted to smack me and whip me good. Yet they just kept on being friends and trying to guide me and point me to Christ. Now I will be there to weather more storms with them.

Are you trying to weather the storm alone? Don't do it. It is too hard. Let your friend or friends go with you. Let them reach out to you. You need them. God made us to share ourselves with others, people we can be real with. So find someone to talk to. I pray God places the desire within each one of us to be the friend we need to be to help someone in need. We are God's hands and feet. Friendships are vital for encouragement, support and protection.

I was listening to a conversation in my connect group at church recently. One lady there is a fairly new Christian. We had a visitor who talked about how she loved to come but couldn't always afford the gas to drive so far. I heard the other one tell her she would come to get her. It was a blessing to my heart to watch her and hear her be Jesus to this stranger.

Today one of our Sunday connect group class members messaged our group and asked us to pray for her. So many answered her and wrote prayers right there. I loved that she asked, and that we all loved being able to go to God on her behalf. Ecclesiastes 4:9-10: *Two are better than one.... for if they fall, one will lift up his companion.* Isn't that great? We need our friends. Take some time to enjoy yours today. Lean on each other. It's a good thing to be a friend and to have a friend.

I was visiting with my friend Stacey for a bit. I was anxious for her to read what I had written so far. She was planning to edit for me and make my grammar correct. We were laughing and talking and she was able to pull my book up on her kindle. The problem was the tiny little writing on the screen. She said, "I can't see THUS far away."(It's the name of my book!) We both just laughed. She is such a nut. I am so thankful that not only has she weathered the tough storm with me but now we can look back together and laugh. We can go forward and one day this will seem just a blur. Friends forever!

LOCKED IN BATTLE WITH OUR FRIENDS

Our Pastor was preaching out of Ephesians about putting on the whole armor of God. I want to share this part with you. He was talking about putting on the breastplate of righteousness. In the time this passage was written when the soldiers went to battle, they had some cool breastplates. Their breastplates were made so they locked to the soldier beside them. Then when the enemy came toward them, together they could charge him and they were stronger to push the enemy away because their armor was locked together. I had never heard of this. I love it, though. You see, two shields are better than one to push back the enemy. My friends, this is how it is in the storms of life. We have to lock together with our sisters and stand strong together to weather these storms that come our way. It isn't the number of friends. It's having the ones who will lock up with you to push the enemy back, friends that will cover you in prayer, and stay the course of the battle. That may be only one other person, but together you can weather the storm and push satan's darts away. I will never forget one friend telling me one day that she was not leaving me. She stood with me interlocked through the battle and what a difference it has made in my life. As did many other friends. Take comfort that wherever you are in the storm of your life, Jesus will send you a friend and together you can weather the storm.

Do not merely listen to the word…do what it says. James 1:22

Jesus, I love You and I thank You for the friendships you have given me through the years. You have provided in every season of my life, friends for me to share that season with. It makes my heart smile when I go back and think of each one of them. They are priceless. Each one has been a pure delight in my life. Sometimes it is hard for me to understand why some are only for certain seasons, but I am not to question You, Lord. Just to thank You for the time we had together. To everything there is a season, even friendship. I thank You for the group of ladies You provided to help me walk through the past several years. You are perfect, Lord; and it is no surprise that You provided the perfect friends to encircle me and help me to get up and live again. I ask You to bless their lives, Lord, each one of them. They each gave up time with others to weather the storm with me. I thank You for their unselfish love for me. They are priceless gems in my life. You only give us the best and I thank You for that. You said that a true friend loves at all times. I have found that to be true. I thank You now for the new friendships You are growing in my life. I ask You to give me an opportunity to be a blessing to each one of them. Help me to see the value of each friendship You have given me. Jesus, You love me so much that You provide exactly what I need, even in friends. May I take good care of these friendships, knowing they are a gift from You. I thank You for the times we have laughed together and cried together; they are all precious times. I ask You to bless them in a mighty way. Give me an opportunity to be a blessing to each one of them, as they have given up so much for me. I will never forget or cease to thank You for each one of them. You have shown me there are great blessings in healthy friendships. I love You so much. I ask that You help me to treasure each friend from the past and those in the present and know they are all gifts from above. I thank You for the friendships yet to come. I need my friends and am so thankful that is how You designed us, to need one another. Thank You for Your blessings on me through friends. I love You, Jesus. In Your matchless name I pray. Amen

- Who are your best friends in this season of life?
- What do you and your friends like to do together?

- Do you and your friends sharpen each other in God's Word?
- Has there been a season in your life where a friend or friends has weathered a storm with you?
- Describe a time when a friendship had to end. Have you been able to deal with the pain of that friendship and forgive if needed?

If there is someone you have hurt or has hurt you in friendship, go to them and ask them to forgive you or just let them know they hurt you and work through that. The friendship may be over but you need to do what is right in God's eyes. If you have tried to talk to them and they refuse, then walk away knowing that you have done all you can and know God will bring you a new friend for this season of life. Thank God for each friend you have and find ways to be a blessing to them. They are treasures from above.

O love of God, how rich and pure! How measureless and strong!
It shall forevermore endure, the saints and angels' song (F.M. Lehman)

CHAPTER 10

God's Redeeming Love

Ultimately God writes our story. I have shared mine with you. I never thought this would be my life. I thought about Peter as I was writing this. Peter was one of the twelve disciples. The Bible says Peter loved Jesus. Jesus told Peter that, *"Upon You I will build my church"* (Matthew 16:18). Peter had spent much time alongside Jesus. When Jesus said to the disciples before He was crucified that all of them would be made to stumble because of Him that night, Peter answered and said, *"Even if all are made to stumble because of You, I will never be made to stumble"* (Matthew 26:33). Jesus then told him, *"You will deny me this night"* (Matthew 26:34) Peter still says, *"Even if I have to die with You, I will not deny You"* (Matthew 26:35). That was how strongly Peter felt about believing in Christ and following Him.

NO ONE PLANS ON TURNING THEIR BACK ON CHRIST

I guess I felt like that to an extent. I never planned to turn my back on Christ. Yet I did. Peter was asked if he was one of the men seen with this Jesus from Galilee, and Peter said he didn't know what the person was talking about. The Bible tells us three times Peter was asked if he were one of Jesus' followers, and each time Peter said he was not! After the rooster crowed for the third time, he remembered that Jesus had told Him he would deny him and though Peter had said he would never deny Jesus, he had. The Bible tells us he went out and wept bitterly. Jesus had been so good to Peter. He questioned why he denied Him, why he turned his back on his Lord? It devastated Peter to think about what he had done. He was stunned that he had turned his back on Christ in the very hour that Jesus was facing death. Yet Jesus was not surprised. He knew this would happen. I am sure Peter wanted to run and never come back. He couldn't forgive himself for his betrayal of his Lord.

I know a little bit of the anguish Peter must have felt. I, too, felt like I had betrayed the Lord after having grown up in a pastor's home, with all the benefits of a good Christian upbringing. I felt the guilt and gut-wrenching shame so heavy upon me as if a pile of rubble had been poured over me and I couldn't get out from under it. I couldn't believe I had been so blind and self-deceived.

EVEN WHEN WE MESS UP, GOD LOVES US

The amazing part of my story is God loves me! He extended grace to me that I didn't deserve, He broke the chains of sin that had me bound; no matter how far I fell His long arm of mercy and grace reached down even further and lifted me out of the miry pit and gloriously restored my life. God, in His great love for us, knew we would need a Savior. So He sent Jesus to this world to be born in a manger. Jesus walked upon the earth for forty years and lived life. He felt the infirmities that we feel. God loves people or He would never have sent His son to earth. Then God knew there had to be a payment for my sin and yours. So that is why Jesus went to the cross. He died a cruel death. He was beaten and mocked for your sin and mine. Just because He loves us! Romans 5:8, *but God shows His love for us in that while we were still sinners, Christ died for us.*

God's Redeeming Love

It is the very nature and being of God to delight in communicating Himself. God has no selfishness, God keeps nothing to Himself. God's nature is to be always giving. In the sun and the moon and the stars, in every flower you see it, in every bird in the air, in every fish in the sea. God communicates life to His creatures. And the angels around His throne, the seraphim and cherubim who are flames of fire-whence have they their glory? It is because God is love, and He imparts to them of His brightness and His blessedness. And we, His redeemed children- God delights to pour His love into us. And why: Because, as I said, God keeps nothing for Himself. From eternity God had His only begotten Son, and the Father gave Him all things, and nothing that God had was kept back. "God is love." —Andrew Murray

My dear friend, God does not care what I did. He doesn't hold my past against me. I got on my knees a long time ago and ask Jesus to forgive me for the things I had done. I begged Him for forgiveness. In that very moment He forgave me because when I was 8 years old I ask Him to be my Lord and Savior. When I did that He gave me the free gift of salvation. And the Bible tells me that forever He holds me in the palm of His hand. When I asked Him to forgive me for not having Him first in my life, He did. He has cast my sin as far as the east is from the west, never to be remembered again. That is a promise to us in His Holy Word. Psalm 103:12 says, *"As far as the east is from the west, so far has He removed our transgressions from us."* God is love!

GOD BRINGS TRUE FORGIVENESS

I felt so much shame when I saw people and I would sit in church and cry during almost every service. Then I would come home and pray and I knew God had forgiven me but still wondered why I felt so much guilt. One Sunday as we sang this song, I felt God lifting the weight off my shoulders:

Thus Far

I come broken to be mended; I come wounded to be healed. I come desperate to be rescued; I come empty to be filled. I come guilty to be pardoned by the blood of Christ the Lamb. And I'm welcomed with open arms; Praise God, just as I am. (Deniece Williams, William Bradbury, Cyril Loris Neil Holland, sung by Travis Cottrell)

I stepped out of my seat with tears streaming down my face and knelt at the altar. As I poured out my heart to God a sweet lady came to pray with me, as I spoke through tears she listened, then she told me that I needed to forgive myself, that God in His great love had already forgiven me. That was it, I needed to forgive me! I realized I was carrying around so much guilt. I was still worrying about going anywhere and seeing someone who knew of my past. I felt so judged by so many. It made me feel so shameful. When I stood that day I felt the weight of the chains falling from me, all of the chains were gone. God had not only shown me His merciful love, but He redeemed my life and restored me. His grace covered all my sins! My countenance was different after that day; my load was lifted by Jesus Christ. Oh how He loves me.

My chains are gone; I've been set free. My God my Savior has ransomed me; and like a flood His mercy reigns. Unending love, amazing grace (Chris Tomlin)

Now that I had forgiven myself, I had to forgive those who had hurt me. It didn't happen overnight. I would say out loud that I forgive_____. I released the one who had hurt me each time I called the name out loud. I began to feel forgiveness in my heart. God was doing a work in my heart and I could feel Him.

Do you need to forgive yourself? Stop right now and ask God to help you with forgiveness. You will never experience true peace until you forgive yourself, and release yourself to move forward. When we live in unforgiveness we are stuck in the past. So today allow yourself to move forward,

142

forgive yourself.

LOVING GOD IS LOVING HIS WORD

I began to hunger for God's Word like never before. I watched Him begin to meet the needs in my life. I was smiling again. God loves me! He really does, and it resounded in every fiber within me. I remember one particular day when my cell phone, which has a verse that pops up every day, revealed I Peter 5:10: *"And after you have suffered a little while, the God of all grace, who has called you to His eternal glory in Christ, will Himself restore, confirm, strengthen, and establish you."* I stared at my phone. I felt the tears come. It was as if God Himself reached down His hand and told me that He had me. He was speaking to me, and here's what was put on my heart:

I am never going to leave you. I want to use you, My daughter. I have been molding you into what I need you to be. You have resisted so it has taken a little longer than planned. But once again You are calling out to Me and seeking My face and trusting Me. You had Me inside you all along. You just got lost on the path. For a time you walked in your ways but now you are ready to walk in My paths again. I am going to place you where I need to use you and watch you flourish. I had had you hidden in the crevice of My hand while you had to rest from the pain and strife, but now you are ready to fly again. I am releasing you once again to work for Me. You are ready now. Keep your eyes on Me and together we will fly. You still have healing that needs to take place, but if you just rest on Me I will daily be restoring you. I will make you who I need you to be. You don't have to worry about the future, I am already there. I have known you since the day I formed you. I knew that you would fall, but I have forgiven you. I am singing over you, My daughter. You are My prized possession! I need you to get up and tell this world what I have done for you. You don't need to feel shameful. You must hold your head up high. You are My daughter, a daughter of the King of all Kings and Lord of all

Lords. I want you to be transparent to a world who needs to see what I did in you. They need to hear about your pain and they need to see My face in you. I need you to tell them about Psalm 103. "Bless the Lord oh my soul and all that is within me bless His holy name." I need you to tell them I healed you, I redeemed your life from destruction, I crowned you with loving kindness and tender mercies, I will satisfy your mouth with good things. I will show you my mercy forever and ever. Show them I am your shield in the time of trouble. I will tread down your enemies. I am full of compassion and am gracious and righteous. Every morning My mercies are new to you. Great is My faithfulness to you. Tell these women I am going to send you to speak to that you are living Psalm 40. I have brought you out of a horrible pit, out of the miry clay, and set your feet upon a rock. I have established your steps. I have put a new song in your mouth. Many will hear and see you and trust in me because of your testimony. Tammy, you are My child, My daughter, I love you!

That is shouting material right there. That is what my God has done for me. He loves me so much. His grace is more than enough! I am overcome with joy and praise to my Lord just reading that paragraph again. I serve a God who forgives and restores. God had redeemed my life from destruction and restored me, and now I heard him telling me He would use my life to show others what redemption truly was.

JESUS RESTORES PETER

Let's go back to the story of Peter. We have to talk about the ending Jesus gave this story. Earlier we talked about how broken Peter was that he had denied Jesus. After Jesus had risen from the dead; He appeared to the disciples. Then He appeared a second time to them. They had been fishing all night and had caught absolutely nothing. Jesus yelled across the water and asked them if they had any food. They answered that they did not; so, He told them to cast their nets on the right side of the boat and they would find some. They did, and the net was so full they couldn't lift it up! They realized at that moment who had been speaking to them. When Peter realized it was Jesus, he plunged into the water to get to Him. I am sure Peter was flying across the water, swimming as fast as he could to get to the One who had died for him. Peter was living with guilt probably at how he had forsaken Jesus at His darkest hour. I can imagine the smile on their faces as Jesus and Peter looked at each other.

They all went to eat with Jesus. They were so thankful to just be in His presence once again. After they had eaten, the Bible tells us that Jesus went up to Peter and asked Peter if he loved Him more than these? Let's look at the scripture and read this story:

"Simon, son of Jonah, do you love Me more than these?"
He said to Him, "Yes Lord, You know I love You."
He said to him, "Feed My lambs."
He said to him a second time, "Simon, son of Jonah, do you love Me?"
He said to Him, "Yes, Lord; You know that I love You."
He said to him, "Tend My sheep."
He said to him the third time, "Simon, son of Jonah, do you love Me?"
Peter was grieved because He said
to him the third time, "Do you love Me?"
And he said to Him, "Lord, You know all things; You know I love You."
Jesus said to him, "Feed My Sheep" (John 21:15-18).

GOD RESTORES AND USES US TO TELL OTHERS OF HIS GREAT LOVE
Jesus says, "Feed my sheep." He says this same thing three times. Jesus was restoring Peter to minister for Him. Jesus didn't hold it against Peter that he had denied Him. He loved Peter and wanted him to know he was forgiven. He also wanted Peter to know that He wanted him to go out and work for His kingdom. I love that picture. The disciple that loved Christ, but denied Him, felt shame, was now restored and Christ was was going to use Peter

to win souls for Him.

We are just like these men. We mess up and think it is hopeless. Then Jesus passes by and reminds us that nothing is impossible or hopeless. He pours His grace, love, and mercy upon us. He uses broken vessels. I am thankful this story was placed in God's Word as a reminder that anyone can fall. Yet it isn't the fall that we need to put our eyes on but rather the work done after the fall when God restores us. Peter used the rest of his life to tell the world about Jesus and His love.

With the prompting of the Holy Spirit, I gave my testimony in my Sunday connect group. One of the ladies told me that today I had smiled, and I hadn't smiled much since I had been in the class; but now I was smiling. I hugged her and left there smiling! People can see the change in us when God restores our lives and we are in fellowship with Him. It was freeing to be able to say out loud where I had been and that it was in my past. I don't have to carry that burden anymore. She could see the change in my face. Shouldn't it be evident to all we see that God is living in us? I felt so free. I had peace that I had not had for many years. I had quit running and once and for all laid my burden down at Jesus' feet, determined to leave it there. This is what grace feels like!!! Oh how often I have sung that old hymn in the past: *"Twas grace that taught my heart to see and grace my fears relieved, how precious did that grace appeared the hour I first believed"* (John Newton). Once again his grace was covering me. It was real in my life. God loves me rang in my heart.

LETTIE BURD COWMAN

One of the devotion books I have that I absolutely love is *Streams in the Desert*. I decided to look up the author and see what her life was about. Her name was Lettie Burd Cowman. As I read about her I saw that she knew the love of God. After 12 years of marriage she and her husband went to Japan as missionaries. They worked alongside another couple and started a mission board. They opened Bible-training institutes in Japan a few years after their arrival. They had a deep burden for the gospel to reach as many people as they could. Her husband began a campaign in 1913 to equip Japan with the gospel within five years. In January 1918, a year after they had to leave because of his health, they received word that about 60 million Japanese were equipped with the gospel. Wow! Her husband's health continued to decline. Watching him suffer so made her suffer as well. It was during this time of suffering that she wrote this devotional book. It was based on the hardships and her fellowship with God during this time. Her publisher didn't feel the book would do well. Yet readers could connect with her because the devotional spoke to those who had difficulty relating their own sufferings with the eternal purpose for the suffering. So rather than letting the storm deter her from her work for Christ, she used this time to share from her heart. After her husband died she found a note he had left her. It said, "Go on with my unfinished task." So despite her grief she began writing a biography about her husband which she hoped to use to launch a worldwide crusade. She spoke whenever she could. She went all over Europe and many other places spreading the gospel. This crusade marked one of the greatest evangelistic efforts in Europe before Nazi Germany took control. This woman worked diligently for her Lord. She has written many publications. She made a choice to spread the love of God. She tried to reach every living creature with the Word of God. She didn't quit living or working for Christ because of the storms of life. She made a difference for all eternity by choosing to share the love of God. I love this story. She knew the love of God. She included this poem, written by an unknown author in Streams in the Desert. I love the words:

Loved! Then the way will not be drear;
For One we know is ever near, Proving it to our hearts so clear
That we are loved.
Loved when our sky is clouded o'er, and days of sorrow press us sore;

Thus Far

Still we will trust Him evermore, For we are loved.
Time, that affects all things below, Can never change the love He'll show;
The heart of Christ with love will flow, and we are loved.

NOTHING CAN SEPARATE US FROM THE LOVE OF GOD

I love that poem. I don't know who wrote it, but its words are great. It reminds me that nothing can separate me from the love of God. Romans 8:38 says: *I am persuaded that neither death nor life, nor angels nor principalities nor powers, nor things present nor things to come, nor height nor depth, nor any other creature thing, shall be able to separate us from the love of God which is in Christ Jesus our Lord.*

Nothing we can do can separate us from God. Isn't that wonderful news? He loves us despite our wicked ways. That is the God I serve. Isn't that reason enough to say that with God I can weather any storm that comes my way because I know it has a divine purpose. That is so hard to say in the midst of the battle, but it's so true. Every storm has a divine purpose. I may not ever see on this earth what the divine purpose was for the storm I just endured; even if I never know, my job is to just trust my loving Lord, knowing He has a plan far greater than anything I could ever know or understand. Who can comprehend the love of God?

Peace with God is only possible because of His unfathomable love for us
—Priscilla Shirer

GOD'S UNCONDITIONAL LOVE

I was reminded as I picked up an old Bible study I did several years back of God's unconditional love for us. This is what it says, "My love for you is great, you will spend the rest of your life trying to comprehend it and not be able to." Isn't that so true? I am still amazed today that He extended His mercy to me, when I didn't deserve His grace and mercy. I totally messed up, yet He loves me so much He forgave me even though I felt so undeserving. So wherever you are in your life today remember that you can't give up because God's love is unconditional and unending. He can see the beginning from the end. He wants us to rest securely in Him and know He has our best interest in mind. That makes the pain I just went through worth it all. I know that because of the storm and the way God used it to mold me, I will be of greater use for Him. I give Him the glory and the praise. I am anchored in His love.

To write the love of God above, would drain the oceans dry. Nor could the scroll contain the whole, though stretched from sky to sky. O love of God how rich and pure, how measureless and strong! It shall forevermore endure the saints and angels song (Frederick M. Lehman).

DO YOU KNOW THE LOVE OF GOD

Do you know the love of God? The love of God is indescribable. It is unspeakable, it is unending, it is unselfish, it is unmerited, it is unconditional. His love is based on His grace! You can never reach a place where God will NOT love you. His love is audacious! Max Lucado writes: *One of the sweetest reasons God saved you is because He is fond of you. He likes having you around. He thinks you are the best thing to come down the pike in quite a while...If God had a refrigerator, your picture would be on it. If he had a wallet, your photo would be in it. He sends you flowers every spring and a sunrise every morning. Whenever you want to talk, He'll listen. He can live anywhere in the universe, and He chose Your heart. And the Christmas gift He sent you in Bethlehem? Face it friend, He's crazy about you!*

The Bible tells us in John 3:16, *For God so loved the world that He gave His only begotten son, that whosoever believeth in Him should NOT perish but have eternal life.* You and I are the *whosoever's* He is referring to here. God's love is unconditional, sacrificial, valuable, personable, and accessible.

Thus Far

The love of God is accessible to "whoever believes in" Jesus—the only Son of God.

Do not merely listen to the word…do what it says. James 1:22

Jesus, Your word tells me over and over that You love me. You died on the cross because You love me. There is nothing I can do that will cause Your love to leave. I thank You for that unconditional love. Love that soothes my doubts and calms every fear. Love that paid for my sin with a cruel death. You were beaten and mocked for me. How can I say thank You for that kind of love. Your love never fails. You are my best friend. You stick to me closer than a brother or sister could. All I had to do was ask You to save me and You did, that very moment. Jesus, I love You. I adore You. Outside of You, I am nothing. My hope is built on You Lord. You paid my debt for me, how can I say thank You for such love as this. There is nothing that will ever separate me from Your love. Your love knows no boundaries. When I am bad, You love me; when I am sad, You love me; when I feel all alone, You are there and You love me. I bow before You today and thank You for this love that is so undeserved. I am in awe that the God who created the heavens and the earth longs to have a relationship with me. Words cannot express my love for You, Lord. I want to live my life for You. All the days of my life I will worship You, and You alone. I love You Lord, and I lift my voice to worship You, Oh my soul rejoice. Take joy my King, in what You hear, may it be a sweet, sweet sound in Your ear. Jesus, name above all names, You are the love of my life. I am crucified with Christ, and yet I live. I live my life to bring You glory and honor. In Your holy and precious name I pray. Amen and Amen!

- Do you know that God loves you?
- Is there a time when you have felt shame and wondered if God loved you?
- Have there been people who made you feel condemned?
- What does Christ say about condemnation in Romans 8:1?
- Have you ever felt that no one loved you?

Read John 3:16-17

Everyday tell yourself that God loves you! It's true. He would have died for you alone! You are worth everything to Him. So know God loves you so very much. Talk to Him everyday and tell Him how much you adore and love Him. He wants to hear from His children. If you do not know the love of God and have never asked Him to forgive you for your sins, do that right now. Email me or call a friend who can talk to you about salvation. He loves us so much that it's free! Smile, knowing the King of all Kings loves you!

You're an overcomer
Stay in the fight till the final round
You're not going under
'Cause God is holding you right now
You might be down for a moment
Feeling like it's hopeless
That's when He reminds you
You're an overcomer, You're an overcomer (David Arthur Garcia)

CHAPTER 11

I'm An Overcomer

I love the Mandisa song, "*Overcomers.*" The one line says, *Whatever it is you may be going through, I know He's not gonna let it get the best of you, You're an overcomer, stay the fight till the final round...* (David Arthur Garcia).

The Bible tells us in John 16:33: *In the world you will have tribulation, but be of good cheer, I have overcome the world.* Our pastor reminded us recently in his sermon that we are not to live a defeated life but to live in victory. We are all going to endure suffering of some kind in this life. The moment that sin entered this world through Adam and Eve in the garden, we were going to have suffering. The only way not to suffer is not to be born.

Romans 8:18: *For I consider that the sufferings of his present time are not worthy to be compared with the glory which shall be revealed in us.*

I remember years ago in Sunday school class a man making a statement that I have never forgotten. He said, "Even if we have to suffer for the rest of our lives on this earth, what is that compared to eternity with Christ?" I have thought of that so many days. If I live to be 85 that is nothing compared to eternity because in heaven there is endless joy, peace, and no more suffering. My suffering here is nothing compared to the future I have waiting in heaven. When Paul wrote this he knew suffering. He had suffered for the sake of the gospel. Yet he could say, it is nothing compared to going to heaven, just the anticipation of going. So I need to count it all joy when I come into tribulations because I can live in victory, knowing even if I don't see the end to the trial here on earth, there will be an end one day in heaven. This life is but a vapor; heaven is the life I am waiting for.

A TRUE OVERCOMER

I think of my friend Leighann when I think about being an overcomer. She has just gone through her second bout with cancer. I met her as she was a few months from ending her chemo treatment. She would have a treatment every other week and for the rest of the week be very weak, sick, and tired. Yet the next Sunday, I would see her at church most weeks. She taught the connect group I was a part of. I am sure many weeks she didn't feel like coming in to teach, yet there she was. Sometimes we would just talk about our week and what God had brought everyone through. She had the most positive attitude. I loved listening to her talk. I was learning that she was trusting in God and had been studying about heaven in case the cancer overtook her body and she was taken from this life. It was a "wow" moment for me, hearing her speak of this. I am sure she had her moments of "Why, God?" Yet all I could see was her deep love for God and how she was trusting Him for whatever was next. That, my friend, is being an overcomer. She is cancer free at this time and is an example to all who meet her of being totally surrendered to Christ and trusting Him each moment for each need that may arise. She always seemed to have a smile on her face even though she was in pain and not sure what the end held. It is evident in her life that God is her source of strength and she is trusting Him and His sovereignty in this and every situation in her life. She lives in victory, not in defeat. She is a true example of an overcomer.

I used to spend my Saturdays going to Mission 615. I love this ministry.

Every Saturday - rain, snow, whatever the weather these people bus in the less fortunate children in our area and love on them for a couple of hours. They have face painting, a bounce house, and then a kid's worship service. After service they give them a sack lunch and take them home, then they bus in about 300 homeless people. The worship service is wonderful and then there is preaching every week. After that they give them a hot lunch and if they need some things they can line up for the clothes closet. It is a wonderful ministry that I am thankful I have been able to be a part of. There are many Saturdays as an altar worker that I have had people come up for prayer that were living very painful lives. It was heart breaking to hear their stories. One gentleman gave a testimony that has stayed with me. He had lost his job, his home and then his family because of choices he had made. He had nothing. He rode the bus there one Saturday and listened to the message. He accepted Jesus as His Savior that day. Christ changed his life! With the help of the people at 615 he found work. He turned his life around and his wife came back to him. They had a place to live and were attending church. He now was helping with Mission 615. He was an overcomer. I love that story, don't you? A life of victory, not defeat!

JESUS IS OUR GREATEST EXAMPLE OF AN OVERCOMER

Jesus is our greatest example of being an overcomer. He came to this earth and walked as a man so He could take our sin to the cross. In the process, there were those who wanted to take His life. Yet, He continued to do as the Father had told Him. He kept spreading His message of hope, not defeat. He went to the cross and died a cruel death. While on the cross, He was mocked. Yet He was not defeated. He then died on the cross and was put in the tomb. We know the end of this glorious story. Up from the grave, He arose! After three days our Lord arose from the grave. Victoriously He lives! Death was defeated; the grave could not hold the King! Victory was His! He has overcome the grave!

Thus Far

Hold on, you're getting stronger everyday
There's no reason, for you to go astray
Don't give in, don't let it bring you down,
You don't have to worry anymore.
We've been made more than conquerors
Overcomers, in this life
We've been made victorious, through the blood of Jesus Christ (Bill and
Jenny Grein).

I love those words. There's no reason to live any other way, except in victory. Romans 8:35 says, *Who shall separate us from the love of Christ? Shall tribulation, or distress, or persecution, or famine....* Is there anything that can separate us? NO!!!! There is nothing that can separate us from His love. There is no mountain too high for God. Whatever you are facing today, He already knows about it. I was reminded as I read His Word this morning that He saw my substance yet unformed and in His book all was written about me. He already knew what I would face in this life before I was conceived. It all has a purpose. I will say it again; I am not defined by my past mistakes, rather I am made new in Christ everyday. Every morning His mercies are new. I can live a victorious life knowing that He knew I would suffer and He has promised I will not be overtaken by my suffering. I am an overcomer!

WE ARE MORE THAN CONQUERORS

Paul goes on to tell us in Romans 8:37, *Yet in all these things we are more than conquerors through Him who loved us. So whatever you are facing, you can live in victory, not in defeat.* You are an overcomer through Christ. Tell yourself that every morning. I am an overcomer. You will have days where you don't want to get out of bed and face the day. So get in the practice of repeating it in your mind: "I am an overcomer." I am an overcomer! I will live in victory, not in defeat."

I John 5:4 says, *For whatever is born of God overcomes the world. And this is the victory that has overcome the world-- our faith.*

The faith of Leighann is what stood out to me. I thought if this woman can have cancer that could possibly take her life and yet walk around smiling and live in victory, so can I. Her strong faith helped me find mine! It's contagious when we live victoriously. We can help someone else see Christ in our lives and help them to know they can overcome the trial they are facing.

The means of victory, the means of overcoming the world is "our faith." What does this mean? Faith comes from hearing, and hearing from the word of God. If we are to overcome, if we are to be everything that God intends us to be then we must give ourselves to the reading and applying of God's Word. We must read God's Word because the power to overcome comes from God. Amen—A W Tozer

THERE IS NO CONDEMNATION IN CHRIST JESUS

Leighann was teaching one Wednesday night and she made a statement that I have thought about so many days since. She was talking about a situation in her own life that had not changed. She said, "Nothing has changed, but everything is better!" That is why I can say, I am free, I'm an overcomer! I still have a lot of junk to deal with in the aftermath of my life, but guess what has changed? My perspective! God has opened my eyes and enlightened me to His Word. God has delivered me from the shame of my past. The Bible tells me in Romans 8:1: *"There is therefore now no condemnation to those who are in Christ Jesus..."* Isn't that a blessed truth? In other words, God doesn't judge me for all the things I've done wrong . There's no reason to walk in shame or bitterness, God has already paid for my sins and yours! God does not condemn me for my past mistakes. He has forgiven me and forever buried them. I am set free! That feels amazing!

The church I attend is a blessing for so many reasons. God placed me in this wonderful congregation for healing; I am sure of this. I remember a Bible Study that sticks out in my mind where a sweet lady told her story to our Wednesday night ladies group. She opened up and was transparent to help others to see that the church isn't full of perfect people who have had no junk in their past. She told her story to help other women to see what God has done in her life. It was a beautiful story! We went around our table afterwards sharing suffering present or past that we had been through. Again, there was great freedom in sharing the past. I didn't share every detail because that isn't necessary, but you understand what I mean. God used all my pain to bring me to a place of freedom in Him. I am so thankful, I can truly say as James did in chapter 1, I count it all joy that I fell into trials because the testing of my faith produced the woman God needed me to be. . It is freeing to be able to say this is what I have lived through and these are some of the mistakes I have made, but now I have overcome.

We also glory in tribulations, knowing that tribulation produced perseverance; and perseverance, character; and character, hope (Romans 5:3-4).

Remember today, we are overcomers! I have victory over sin. I will not live in defeat but in victory. I will fight the fight knowing it isn't a hopeless fight. Jesus is living in me. He overcame death on the cross, and He is who I look to as I claim victory. I can think of so many friends I know who have overcome cancer, alcohol, drugs, pornography, and so many other things. They are overcomers! I want others to see Christ in me; I am an overcomer. I am so happy that God has given me this great victory. No trial is in vain. They all have a purpose in our lives. We just have to live as overcomers even when we don't know what the end of the trial looks like. We can live victoriously knowing our God knows the end, and that is all that matters! We don't have to know everything, but we have to hold on to the One who does! So claim it today. Victory is yours for the claiming! I am an overcomer!

*** Pray * Ponder * Praise ***

Do not merely listen to the word,,,do what it says. James 1:22

Jesus, my Lord and Savior, I just want You to know I love You. When I felt overwhelmed, You came to me and reminded me that through You I could overcome anything that came my way. You overcame death on the cross for me. You are my refuge and a very present help in time of trouble. You will carry me when I cannot walk. There is nothing I cannot overcome through You. You are for me! I can live victorious in You, Lord. Knowing that the testing of my faith produces Godliness, You are perfecting me through the trials into Your image. Knowing this I can overcome anything that comes my way. I am walking hand in hand with You, Jesus. You have not given me a spirit of fear but a spirit of love and power and a sound mind. I know whom I have believed and I am persuaded that You will keep me until I see You face to face that glorious day. I will lie down in peace, knowing that You know my way; and when I am tried, I will come forth as pure gold. I am not going to give up; I am an overcomer through You, Lord Jesus. Satan get away from me; I will not be overcome with sin, but sin will be overcome by the power and the blood of Jesus Christ. I have given it all to You, God, and I know You have delivered me; so satan needs to back away from me. I am a daughter of the King. You are keeping watch over me. I trust You, Lord, with my life. I live to please You. Thank You for showing me I could overcome through You. I love You and I am honored to be Your vessel. In Your name I pray. Amen and Amen!

- What obstacle have you had to overcome?
- Has satan tried to tell you that you could not overcome?
- Do you feel right now there is no reason to try?
- Read Romans 8:37.
- Are you in the middle of the battle?
- Are you an overcomer?

Then live in victory. Smile and thank God for helping you overcome. He is a gracious God full of mercy and love. He will help us overcome anything that comes our way. Remember, He is for us! Don't walk around feeling

161

defeated. Walk boldly in victory today. Even if you are in the midst of the battle, God knows the end and He wins every time! So you will overcome! That is how we can have joy in the midst of the journey. I know that in the end God wins every time! I trust Him today and always.

All the way my Savior leads me, what have I to ask beside?
Can I doubt His tender mercy, Who through life has been my guide?
Heavenly peace, divinest comfort, Here by faith in Him to dwell!
For I know what-e'er befalls me, Jesus doeth all things well (Fanny J. Crosby)

CHAPTER 12

The New Me

When my girls and I are riding down the road we are usually listening to music. Either we have the radio on singing along or my daughter will plug her phone in and play her music. There is a song that they listen to that I thought of this morning. *"This is real, this is me, I'm exactly who I'm supposed to be now..."* (Demi Lovato)

Well, this is me, the new me! I am in a new phase of life. Sometimes I am not sure about this new me; she is still finding her way. I am strong in Christ and very anchored in His Word, but life is different. It will never again be the same. That is hard to swallow, isn't it? I hate change! Some days I feel like I am a tight rope walker and I have gotten to the middle but I am scared to keep going. I don't know about this new life some days. Friends remind me I still have the scabs on my wounds right now. I am well aware of that. Yet life has to move on, back to some kind of normal.

WHO AM I NOW

If you, like myself, have been through an event that forever changed your life, it's sometimes hard to figure out who you are and what you are supposed to do now? Each morning when I pray, I normally end my prayer like this,

"God, please go before me this day. I don't know what this new day holds, but I know You do; so I ask you to guide me and show me the way."

Even though I have come to the other side of the trial and I am so content and happy in Christ, there are many changes in my life. The biggest change is that I spend much time alone. Even though I was in an unhealthy marriage, there is something to be said about just the contact you have with the other person. I think it's what keeps people in unhappy marriages. You are scared of what it will be like to be totally alone. I get it! I am there. I have Jesus and He is my best friend, but I am human and get lonely. Now that fall is here, I do love some nights to put on my pj's and snuggle up on the couch with a good book. I love to read, and for the past two years I had not been able to stay focused long enough to read an entire book. So that is one way I am using my time.

BEING ALONE AND BEING LONELY

I had a friend over for dinner last night. She was talking about the difference between being alone and being lonely. She knows how that feels. She is married and her husband is out of town this week. She likes the days to go home and catch up on things because she knows he is coming back and she can get through the times alone, just knowing that. Loneliness is different. No one is coming back! This is the new normal.

God brought a dear sweet young lady into my life and has allowed me to use what I have been through to help her with where she is in life right now. She is a source of pure joy in my life! We pray together many days and love to sing together. It is an amazing feeling to know God is using my past to be able to relate to where she is. I am watching God help her mend and give her wings to fly again. I am so thankful God allowed our paths to cross! I love you and I love watching how God is working in your life!

Most of my girlfriends are married. I hate to call them at night because I know they are having family time. The friend I do have that is single works late and is usually tired. So I am learning how to spend my time. Yet I must tell you, I am very content on my own. I have found I enjoy some time alone to read God's Word, and be content in who I am. I don't need to date to find happiness, I am happy right where I am, single. Christ is my dearest friend, and He has given me such peace in singleness. I love my life!

My ex-husband and I share custody of our two younger girls. So I have had to get used to sharing my girls with their dad. I want them to be able to spend time with him. I know it is so important. However, we do try to have family meals for birthdays and big events. We are both cordial to each other; we just don't want to be married. Yet we have four precious children to continue to rear together. They must be our priority. So we work together for our family. Even with all that, it's still divorce and it stinks most days. So I have days without the girls now to get used to. I was a stay-home Mom for 19 years where my daily life consisted of taking care of children full time. So it is very different now, especially when they are not here. But I am learning to deal with loneliness.

I am also learning to deal with the fact that I have to pay my bills. This is a biggie for me. It is very scary to be the bread winner. Yet God has provided my every need every month. I love my job, and my boss is amazing. I am financially secure on my own. Thank you, Jesus, is all I can say. Sometimes I have to remind myself God is in control. In my devotion time this morning I was reminded by this statement that God is enough: *"Do not linger in the future because anxieties sprout up like mushrooms when you wander there"* (*Jesus Calling*, October 17). That's true, isn't it? If I sit here alone and think about how I am going to pay my bills next month, or if the car breaks down, or if the central unit tears up, then what am I going to do. Before long, I have worked myself into feeling so much pressure. We have to take one day at a time. I will assure you I will continue to worry some; it's just natural and so will you. Yet I can tell you God has supplied every need I have had. He has supplied them in ways I couldn't even see.

We had an old camper that we loved to go camping in several years back.

We decided we needed to sell it because we just didn't use it anymore. At that particular time I really didn't know how I would pay my house payment. I knew I could ask my mother, but I hated to. I began to pray. I got up one day and cleaned that camper out top to bottom. I took pictures and put it on Facebook for sale. When it didn't sell there, I put it on another website and the next day someone came and paid cash for it. God will supply your needs. Philippians 4:19 reminds us, *My God WILL supply all your need according to His riches in glory by Christ Jesus.* So just remember not to spend time in your chair worrying about tomorrow. I know that is easier said than done. This old quote says it all: *"Today is the tomorrow, I worried about yesterday"* (Dale Carnegie). We have to take one day at a time and not look to the future right now.

MOVING FORWARD

Not only do I have to get used to the loneliness and being the bread winner, but I have to embrace being alone. For the first time since I was 19 years old, I am on my own, alone. It can be scary. There are many times people will still ask me how my ex-husband is and I just answer. It seems to be easier than telling them I am divorced. I still remember my first big event to attend after my divorce; it was my best friend's son's wedding. I was really nervous. My children knew I was. The girls sat with me and another friend came to sit with me. It is different just being alone. I felt a little awkward. Sometimes people don't know what to say to me. They hug me but there is that awkward conversation. I want to tell them I am still me, just a new version. Hey, we all need updating, don't we? I kind of like that. I am an updated version of me. I knew I had to go my son was in the wedding. I wouldn't have missed it for the world. So I made the best of it. When I got to the reception, I couldn't find a place to sit and I began to feel a little panic inside. My children went to sit with their friends and my little girl was riding over with her brother and they hadn't arrived yet. I went outside to pray, wanting to leave immediately; but I knew that this was something I needed to attend. I needed to be there for my friend and her family. So I sucked it up, went back in, took my seat, and ate my meal. In the end, I was of course, fine. You will survive if you are dealing with being alone.

DIVORCE IS NOT A DIRTY WORD

I have had to learn about the word divorce. I have had to learn that it is not a dirty word. It is where I am. I am divorced. I am a single mom. Right before my divorce I purchased a book that was really helpful to me. It was called, *The Single Life Mom*, by Angela Thomas. It helped me see what I was feeling was normal. She, too, had experienced fear and anxiety because she was now single. It was very helpful to me as I began a new journey that was very unfamiliar for me. I am surviving being divorced. I am not an advocate for divorce, but it's where I am. I can tell you I do feel that it was more wrong for me to be living a lie and always covering than it is to be divorced and be real. I believe that. I know many great Christian people who are divorced. I have many role models in my life and they have been through divorce. It doesn't define you or set you apart.

I don't believe there is a section in heaven marked, "Divorced people, come this way." No, that is crazy, so we shouldn't think like that here either. I don't think God loves divorce; but as I stated earlier, He does love people and forgives all. Do I love it—no! Definitely not. I didn't go into marriage thinking one day I would be divorced. I went into marriage saying this is it forever. I have had to deal with the fact that my marriage didn't last forever. It doesn't mean I am labeled or he is labeled; it simply means our marriage had so many issues that forever was impossible for us. I have resigned to the fact that it's okay. So I have had to face the fact that when I go out in public I can say I am single, I am divorced and the earth will not rip apart.

My number one priority right now is making sure my children are okay. Divorce is hard on everyone. I pray for each one of them many times a day.

I see my youngest, especially, sometimes acting nervous. I don't want them to feel guilty for wanting to see their Dad or wanting to see me. We really try to allow them to call the other one or stop by and see them, if they are on a long visit. I want them to be as okay as they can be in divorce. My oldest two go back and forth when they are home from college. I know it is hard on them as well. Our home is forever changed.

HELPING THE KIDS KNOW WHAT NORMAL LOOKS LIKE

I want them to be able to have a normal relationship when they begin to date. My oldest son just got married. We have talked often about how important it is for him to hold her hand and show her affection. They didn't see that in our home, so I want them to know what a girl wants. That is important to me as we move on. I often worry about them because I have heard my boys share how they knew our home wasn't normal. One said when he would go to his friend's house and see his parents and he knew that our home wasn't normal. So now I pray and encourage each one of them who is ready to date how they need to treat their dates. That is important to me. I don't want to see them hurt or them hurt someone else because of our home life. Sometimes I wish I had left many years ago, yet I know God's timing is always perfect.

Another way I am finding the new me is in ministry opportunities. Now that I am ready to move on, I need to find a way to pour myself into something else. I have always enjoyed serving in the church. I am at a new church, so I'm learning my way as I go. It's like starting over. Church has always been a vital part of my life. I love my church; it's a great big family. For a time, I enjoyed that I could come in and worship and leave. No one knew me and I could heal slowly without feeling pressure from those who loved me. Now I am ready for the next phase which is serving in some capacity. One way I am serving is by singing in the choir.

A few years back, I received a message asking me to come play the piano at one of the local nursing homes for service once a week. At first I thought, no, I don't have time. At the time, I was working full time. Yet as I prayed, I felt it was a way for me to begin to give again. I love to play the piano and was used to playing every week at church. So I decided I would enjoy playing again. I actually loved this ministry. I was the one who walked away blessed each week. I love hearing the old folks sing the old hymns. It's amazing how those words stay in our minds, even when we can't remember many other things.

One day my little girl was out of school so I took her with me to the nursing home. It turned out that the lady who leads the singing wasn't coming. My daughter stood beside the piano with her hymn book and led the crowd with the help of another lady. It was a blessing to me and to the older people. They loved watching her sing. It was a way I could see she was beginning to learn to serve. My heart swelled with joy as I watched her. Well, the man who was speaking didn't show up, so I spoke. I felt very nervous for a minute and out of practice. But as soon as I opened my mouth God gave me the words to say that day. I spoke to them about waiting and being patient. It was perfect for them and for me.

FINDING A NEED AND MEETING IT, FINDING A HURT AND HEALING IT

Who would have thought God would use a nursing home to show me He could and would use me again. I went back to play again and a few of them told me they really loved my playing. One lady spoke up and said, "Tammy, you did a great job speaking last week." I just sat there and had to smile and sad "Thank you, God." This new "me" has for so long tried to figure out how God could use me again. He showed me He hasn't changed; and though my life is very different, I too am the same lady who loves to serve my God however He sees fit.

Since I first began writing this book, I have had the opportunity to speak and sing many times. Each time I am humbled as my Lord uses me once again. Whether it's behind the piano or speaking to a crowd, it is pure joy to be able to serve in this way once again. God is opening many doors to show me He desires to use us and our stories to bring people to Him.

INTIMACY WITH CHRIST

God continues to show Himself every day in new ways to me. I feel in this new "me" phase of life such a deep, intimate relationship with Christ. I love the verse in Habakkuk 3:17: *"Though the fig tree may not blossom, nor fruit be on the vines; though the labor of the olive may fail, and the fields yield no food; though the flock may be cut off from the fold, and there be no herd in the stalls, yet I will rejoice in the Lord, I will joy in the God of my salvation. The Lord God is my strength, He will make my feet like deer's feet, and He will make me walk on my high hills. We could replace part of this verse and make it sound like this, though I lose my husband to death, though I have cancer, though I am left alone and suffering, whatever your though is, though I lose everything I have, YET I WILL REJOICE IN THE LORD, I WILL JOY IN THE GOD OF MY SALVATION.* "Habakkuk's love for God was not based on what God would give him or what he had. *Even if God sent him suffering and loss, he resolved to rejoice not in the situation but in the Savior, who is sovereign and would be his strength"* (Women's Study Bible). This is how I want to be, rejoicing no matter what I might have lost and even though my pain is still great. My joy is in Christ.

THE STORY OF DORCAS

One of the stories that intrigues me in the Bible is in Acts chapter 9. This chapter tells a small part of the story of the life of a woman named Dorcas. She was a beautiful lady who left her homeland and came to live among the Greeks. The Bible doesn't tell us why she left her familiar surroundings, but this was right around the time Saul was killing Christians. What would make her leave everything she knew and travel to a place where even the language was different? You talk about change! That is a big change. Whatever the reason was and whatever pain she might have left behind, the Bible is clear that she came to this town and began to serve. Her ministry was making shawls of some sort or clothing for the widows of Joppa. The widows became her ministry. Most of the men worked at sea where accidents were common and would leave many women without husbands. Dorcas had compassion on these women. I can imagine she may have opened up her home to them. My point is that she found a ministry and focused on ministering to them and making a difference for Christ. She didn't move there and stay in her home, living in fear and crying about the change. She got up and said, "Okay, this is a new phase of life, and I am going to find good in it." That is my own interpretation. I am sure she had days of missing her family and the life she had left behind. She was human. Yet she pushed through the pain and focused outward on others. She became sick and died; and the Bible says that all the women came and wept and were so saddened by her death. Peter happened to be near there and was called to come to her home. When he came in, all the women were crying and showing him the beautiful garments Dorcas had made for them. Peter sent them out and knelt down and prayed. That day she was raised from the dead! Can you imagine the women's joy when she walked out of the room alive! God was not through with her yet. He took great joy in her life that she was giving for others. I am sure the news spread quickly of the miracle. I love this story. All she did was minister with what she had and God used her in a mighty way.

The Bible did not focus on her past but on the present. Life is not about our past; it's about what we going to do now with what we have been given. It doesn't matter about Dorcas' past; what matters is the way she lived her life for the rest of it. That is what our Lord chose for us to read about in His Word. What does that say to you and me? That God wants to focus on the here and now. How will we use the present to impact others for Him? We have to leave the past behind and focus on where we are now.

LIVING IN THE PRESENT

The Bible talks about forgetting what is behind us and pressing forward toward the prize... There are days that I will sit and think about what I am supposed to do now. There will be many days of mourning the past. That is just normal life. The grieving process takes time, so let yourself grieve whatever it is that you have lost. Know that it is okay. But we have to begin to find where God can use us again. We have to live in the present.

I was watching a video someone posted on my Facebook wall . It was wonderful; I have had the song in my mind all afternoon, and it is very fitting for this chapter.

> *I am redeemed, you set me free! So I'll take off these heavy chains*
> *Wipe away every stain, now I'm not who I used to be, I am redeemed!*

I love the second verse because it reminds me that I, too, have had so much shame and regret that I have carried from my past, but now I am laying it down and walking away. The verse says:

> *All of my life I have been called unworthy*
> *Named by the voice of my shame and regret, but when I hear You whisper,*
> *"Child lift up your head," I remember, oh God, You're not done with me*
> *yet! (Mike Weaver and Benji Cowart)*

He isn't done with me yet, praise His Holy Name. I will never be the same again, but that is okay because He wants to use me now. He has equipped me even more to work for Him. The song has another line I absolutely love! Listen to this verse and rejoice with me:

The New Me

Because I don't have to be the old man inside of me, cause his day is long dead and gone
Because I've got a new name, a new life, I'm not the same
And a hope that will carry me home,
I am redeemed!

Those are words of victory. I can be excited about where I am in life. I am not who I was, but thank God I am redeemed! I love it! So now I just have to get up and pray and seek God and see how and where He needs to use me. I am His vessel and willing to go and do whatever He has for me.

So remember, none of us likes change. I was married for almost 25 years. I have days where it is really hard. I am sure there are many more hard days to come, but I will hold my head up and trust my almighty God to guide me through this "new" phase of life. I will hold my head up with confidence, knowing He has a plan far greater than you or I could possibly fathom.

One morning my devotion time took me to Ephesians 3:20-21. Let's quote this together, *Now to Him who is able to do exceedingly abundantly above all that we ask or think, according to the power that works in us, to Him be glory... Forever and ever. Amen.*

Through the power at work in us God can accomplish anything He might purpose. Through us the world could hear the Gospel and come to the knowledge of the truth; through us God can advance any of His prerogatives powerfully. As the Creator, He can do all that can be done, what we can imagine and well beyond that. Like Shadrach, Meshach, and Abednego, we must never doubt God's ability. I'm praying with anticipation at what God can and will do with my life.

He is able to bring us to a happy place in life, a place that overflows with His abundant grace and rich mercy. He has brought me through a storm that I thought would kill me. Christ bestowed grace to me even when I didn't deserve it. You like me, might feel beaten down by the hard waves you have endured. But know this; He is not through with you yet. Smile and thank God for this "new" person He has been molding.

This is real, this is me, I'm exactly who I'm supposed to be now...

*** Pray * Ponder * Praise ***

Do not merely listen to the word...do what it says. James 1:22

Dear Jesus, it's me again! I am so glad to call You friend. I am a friend of the almighty God. Wow! Lord, I am amazed by You and how You love me. I am in awe of how you are molding me and making me who You need for me to be. I am not who I used to be, but I am who You created me to be. I can truly say I count it all joy that I fell into all kinds of trials; because the testing of my faith has produced a woman who looks nothing like who I used to be. You are perfecting that which concerns me. I know it's only through the fire that You were able to mold me. So I thank You today for the fire I went through. I thank You for the ones that will come my way in the future. I know that you walk before me and know everything that will come my way. Now this new woman is confident in You and Your power. I will walk in obedience. I am forever changed. I never want to go back to who I once was. I thank You for reminding me from time to time what You have brought me through and are showing me how You had the perfect plan. I just had to trust You. You have brought me into such an intimate relationship with You Lord. If it took the trials to draw me closer to You, then I thank You for them. You are my all in all. You are all I need. You have been so faithful to me. I hardly know how to thank You. I am filled with such gratitude to You. It's like You just picked me up and placed me on a rock until I was strong enough to begin to walk again. So many nights I just sat and cried to You and told You I didn't even know the words to pray, so You just held me and prayed over me. I could feel Your presence with me. Thank you, Jesus, for surrounding me with Your love. You have drawn me out of the waters that wanted to consume me and hid me in the shelter of Your wings until I could fly again. Now I am ready to spread my wings. God show me the path You would have me to walk and help my eyes to stay focused only on You, Jesus. May I not look to the left or to the right, but only keep my eyes on You. You have filled me with such unspeakable joy. Here I am; do with me whatever You please. I am Your servant. I will do whatever You ask of me. Thank You for Your grace and mercy that carried me thus far. I love You, my wonderful Lord. I can never thank You enough for giving me the life I have in You. Search me daily and may I always seek to remove those things that are unpleasing to You. It's in Your name I pray, the name above all names, the name of Jesus. Amen!

- What is new in your life?
- Are you at a place to be thankful for this new thing, whatever it may be?
- How have you been changed in the process?
- Can you see how through the fire God had a purpose in mind?
- What has God shown you about the "new you"?

Cradled in my arms, I held you
And I loved you more with each day passing by; sharing joy, sharing pain
Through the sunshine and the rain, I can't believe how quickly time's gone by
I don't know what the future brings you, but I hope that you'll keep heaven as your goal
For we've taught you how to pray; we made sure you knew the way
So remember my request before you go
Just be there, when I finally make it home; and I stand before the throne, just be there
When I look around to see if you are standing next to me, just be there (Paula Gray)

CHAPTER 13

My Legacy

As I was drawing this book to an end, it seemed to need this one last chapter. Do you ever think how your story, your legacy, is going to be told in generations to come if Christ doesn't come back soon? What is a legacy? Legacy is your inheritance. Legacy is your gift to the world. I began to think what would my legacy be? What would I leave behind?

When I think on the stories in the Bible of Paul, Moses, Peter, Jonah, and others, it isn't their mistakes that stick out in my mind. It is the way they allowed God to use them after they messed up that stands out to me. Their past did not define them, and neither does mine. This made me think on the story of my life. How will it be interpreted after I am gone?

You shall love the Lord your God with all your heart and with all your soul and with all your might. And these words that I command you today shall be on your heart. You shall teach them diligently to your children, and shall talk of them when you sit in your house, and when you walk by the way, and when you lie down, and when you rise. Deuteronomy 6:5-7

When my children grow up and are talking to their children about me, I want it to be a story of a grandmother who was a woman of strong faith.

She spent her life telling others about Jesus. She gave the message of hope to everyone she came into contact with. I don't want my story to be that your grandma started out strong but took a turn for the worse and never recovered. She lived the rest of her days hiding in her home, filled with bitterness and anger.

God desires for all to tell this world about Him. It's through our stories we do this. You may be able to reach a people that others can't because of what you have been through. You may say, "I have no story." We all have a story. We must learn to be transparent and open up and share. Our stories are part of our legacy.

When I read about Kay Arthur's life it was so similar to mine. I could relate to every word I was reading. God used her story to encourage me, and help me know I could make it; because of this, I wanted to include her story in my book for you to read. Her great boldness for Christ and her willingness to be transparent, helped me when I felt called to share my story.

Kay Arthur's Story

Kay was brought up in a home that honored God. She had a family who loved and respected each other. She believed, "Of course I'm a Christian. I live in the United States, and I go to church." She came to realize later in life that what she knew then was a religion, not a relationship.

Because Kay admired her parent's marriage, she longed for the day she would marry too. Kay married the man she thought would be the fulfillment of all her dreams. She was warned that things might not be as they appeared, but pride became her guide. He gave her a huge diamond ring, and was most certainly her Prince Charming.

Kay and Tom were blessed with two precious sons, but her marriage was far from perfect. Battling with depression, he was unable to find stability in a career. As much as Tom had going for himself, Kay could not understand why he struggled. She wanted to enjoy life, even if it meant doing so on her own.

Kay admits that she did not love her husband unconditionally. Neither had she tried to understand him. She wanted to be happy. She wanted her needs satisfied. Only later did Kay really realize that wasn't what love was about. Seeking the guidance of their minister, they were advised to divorce. Regretfully, Kay recalls that the Word of God was never even opened in that counseling session. After just six years, their marriage came to an end.

She remembers being warned, "Sin will take you farther than you ever intended to go, it will cost you more than you ever expected to pay, and it will keep you longer than you ever intended to stay." This became true of Kay's life for the next few years as she began seeking comfort in other men, at one point having a two-year relationship with a married man. Going from one man to the next, she was always looking for someone, anyone who would unconditionally love her.

Then suddenly, one day she became aware of the emptiness in the life she was leading. "I realized that someday I would stand before a holy God, and He would say, 'Depart from Me!'" At first she decided she would try to be good, but the good she wanted to do she couldn't do. "The evil that I didn't want to do, I did. I thought, 'If I could just erase my past. If I could just have a new start.'"

At a party one evening in 1963, a friend said to Kay, "Why don't you quit telling God what you want and tell Him that Jesus Christ is all you need?" The next morning, Kay stood before God and said, "God I don't care what you do to me. I don't care if I never see another man as long as I live. I don't care if you paralyze me from the neck down. I don't care what you do to my two boys." Those were the worst things she could conceive of having happen to her. "God, if you'll just give me peace!" God at that moment gave Kay Arthur the Prince of Peace, His Son, Jesus Christ. He called her "Beloved" when she knew there was nothing lovely about her. "I went down on my knees a harlot, and I got up a saint."

(Taken from an article in *Just Between Us* by Laurie Beyer)

Kay Arthur is a teacher, host, author, and founder of Precept Ministries International

If you have done any of Kay Arthur's studies as I have, you hear and know her love for Christ in every word. There are countless lives she has touched just by sharing her story, by choosing to allow God to use her transparency for His glory. What a legacy of faith.

A LEGACY OF FAITH

I go back to the story of my father. In only ten years he had taught me the ways of Christ by demonstrating them to me. He had an altar in the woods where he would go to pray. We would drive there and I would stay in a certain spot and play while he went back and prayed. I will never forget that. Now he wasn't perfect. I know of his past and there were times I heard him speak of his regrets. My point is that he left me a legacy of Christ. I know without a doubt that Christ was number one in his life. The ending of his story is that he lived a faithful life and followed hard after Christ and sought to tell everyone he saw about this Jesus he had met, and how He changed his life.

My mom has the same story. She has left such a legacy of faith. My mom was a quiet humble woman. She loved the Word of God, and was constantly reading and marking her Bible. I remember telling her about a situation where I wanted to speak my mind to someone who I felt had wronged me. My mom's response was, "You need to remain quiet and pray, let God take care of the situation." She was a wise woman of prayer. She spent the last 5 years of her life going to dialysis four days a week. The nurses there would tell you she rarely complained and always had a smile on her face. She was kind to everyone she came in contact with. She was a true example of Proverbs 31, "Her children rise up and call her blessed ..." Two weeks before her death she had been in church. She would walk down the aisle, very slowly carrying her oxygen tank. What a strong faith in God I saw in my sweet mother. My mom went to see Jesus a year ago. During the last minutes of her life I held her hand and sang to her, "When we all get to heaven, what a day of rejoicing that will be. When we all see Jesus, we'll sing and shout the victory." I told her, "Tell daddy I'm coming, I will see you both soon."

My parents have left a strong legacy of faith for our family. I want to leave that same legacy of faith for my children to tell their children. **A story of redemption**. I have made numerous mistakes. Yet God redeemed my life and I pray He will use my story to bring others to Him. I want that to be my legacy. I love this song sung by Nichole Nordeman:

I want to leave a legacy, How will they remember me?
Did I Choose to love? Did I point to You enough
To make a mark on things, I want to leave an offering
A child of mercy and grace, Who blessed Your name unapologetically
I want to leave a legacy (James Newton Howard)

That is my prayer. As you read my story, I pray you walk away feeling you met a lady who knows Jesus and is making a difference for Him. That is the most important thing to me in telling my story. That lives are touched and hope is seen in my story. I want to leave a legacy of faith.

God has richly blessed me with four wonderful children. I want them to know the love of Christ. I want it to be demonstrated in my life. The past few years have been very hard on them. I know that. I hear their pain sometimes. It breaks my heart that they have had to endure this road also. Yet I know God is putting us back together even better than before. They see their mom laughing again and know Christ is my dearest friend. I pray they see Him in my eyes, and hear Him in my voice and see Him in all that I do. I want to leave a legacy of grace and redemption for them to see.

MANY WILL BELIEVE BECAUSE OF ONE WOMAN'S TES-TIMONY

As I was cleaning my piano room the other day, I found a devotion I had written for a Bible study I was teaching. I read this first line and it brought tears to my eyes. I taught this and wrote this many years before the trial I just went through. Isn't it something when we see how God was preparing us for the battle? It was the story of the woman at the well. The first line I wrote says, *Many believed because of one woman's testimony*. That is my prayer as I write this. That many will believe because of my testimony. I want

Christ to use my words to show you that God loves you and desires for you to see that His love is greater than any trial we face. We don't always get an answer for why we are going through the storm. We just need to know that God loves us and longs for us to just trust Him and show Him our love by demonstrating His faith in our lives.

You may be facing sickness, or maybe you have lost someone dear to you, lost a job, or facing a divorce or dealing with depression. Maybe you are addicted to drugs, alcohol, or pornography. Maybe you are having an affair. I don't know where you are, but I pray you see that God desires to bring you through the storm and use your story. A story doesn't have to have a fairytale ending. God writes the ending. His grace is enough. Draw near to Him and He will draw near to you. I would love to tell you my story has this great fairytale ending. But actually Prince Charming has not ridden up on a white horse to get me and I haven't hit the jack pot. But you know what? I'm a millionaire, I'm rich in Christ. I am not through yet. God is still writing my story. He is my Prince. I desire to honor Him with my life. He is teaching me that He wants to give me abundantly more than I had ever hoped, dreamed or imagined, as it says in Ephesians. I am excited to see what He has in store for me. My joy is in my Lord. My life is so full in Christ. I do not need anything else. He is the love of my life; He is my best friend. I long each day to see what He is going to do. I smile right now, knowing He is up to something and I can't wait to see what it is.

I pray that He has used my story to speak to your heart, to encourage you along your way, to show you there is hope is Christ. I can't wait to run into His arms someday and see Him face to face. Until then I will keep letting Him write my story. I will keep sharing my faith, and I pray to leave legacy of faith in Christ. I believe as it says in John 4:39, ***Many will believe because of ONE woman's testimony.*** This is my story, *thus far...*

Perfect redemption, All is at rest
I in my Savior am happy and blest

My Legacy

I'm watching and waiting, looking above
Filled with His goodness, and lost in His love
This is my story, this is my song
Praising my Savior, all the day long (Fanny Crosby)

*** Pray * Ponder * Praise ***

Do not merely listen to the word…do what it says. James 1:22

My gracious, heavenly Father, I come to You, thanking You for the life You have given me. I not only thank You for the family I was born into but the family You have blessed me with. I thank You for my four children. What a great God You are. I am so blessed. Take each one of their lives and use them in a mighty way for Your kingdom. I pray that each one of them can see Your light in me. Help me to always walk in Your ways, knowing they are watching me. May they forgive me for the pain they each endured because of my choices. Help me to keep them in mind as I daily am faced with many other decisions. May I always live in obedience to You, knowing obedience is the only way to live. Lord, I want to leave a legacy of faith behind me. I thank You for the legacy of faith I was born into. May I never take for granted what You have so blessed me with. I want Your light to shine so brightly in me that I am like the city burning on the hill. May I never lose the desire to serve You. I pray the grandchildren that are yet to come will live to know of Your ways in our family. When I stand in heaven, Lord, may I look around and see all of my children standing there with me. That will be my greatest reward. When I leave this world, may those I leave behind know I was a woman of faith who loved You above all else. I want to leave a mark for You, Lord, on this earth when I am gone. I can't wait for the day I will see You face to face. When I finally bow before You and can truly thank You for who You are. May I live each day as if it were my last. Fill me with love and laughter, where all around me are blessed, knowing who lives in me. You are my song in the night, You are the love of my life. Jesus I am so in love with You. I sit here now with my head bowed, thanking You without words for all You are to me. Thank you for the journey we have walked hand in hand. I would not be who I am today without the storms. I can't wait to see where you take me next. I am excited, knowing You are able to do exceedingly and abundantly more than I could ever dream. I am ready for the journey with You, my Lord. Thank you for lives You have entrusted to me. May I live so they can know who I live for. Thank You for the story You have written on my heart. I haven't always been thankful for this journey. I now can say I am ready for the new things You are doing in my life. I am not going back to the former things, but I know You are doing a new thing. You will make a road in the desert if that is where You want me to go. I am following You, Lord. From here and forevermore, it's You and me, together. Thank You for my journey, thus far... I took life into my hands and veered off the path, but You pulled me back to You. Thank You so much for loving me. I love You, Lord. In Your powerful name I pray. Amen!

- What are you leaving behind?

I just want to make a mark; I just want to turn someone's heart
In this world, Lord Jesus for You
May I ever burn with Your fire; And never let me lose that desire
To make a mark on this world for you (Rhonda Spurrell c. BMI)

CHAPTER 14

How to Share Your "Thus Far" Story

I feel we live in a culture that says when you go through a raging storm, it is better to just forget about it and never mention it again. If you don't talk about it, you will forget and people will forget and everyone can just move on and act like nothing happened. I don't believe that is God's way. We are to live a transparent life and know that everything that comes into our lives has a God-given purpose.

I have told you my story to encourage you along your way. The truth is we all have a story of what we have come through thus far. In time I will have more to tell you about my *thus far* journey. So what has grace brought you through, my friends? No matter how small or how big you think it is, God can use it. It may be to encourage your neighbor, or a friend at work, or your group at church. I don't know how God can use your story, but I know He wants to. Nothing that comes into our lives is without purpose. Everything we encounter in this life we can use to help another.

SHARING YOUR STORY

I want to encourage you to share your story. You may not want to write a book, but you could journal your story. You could start by sharing your story with a friend. Then pray and ask God to place someone along your path that you could minister to because of what you have been through. Or you may want to share your story with a small group of women. Pray how God could use your "thus far" experiences to help others.

JOURNALING TO HEAL

Journaling is a great way to heal if your journey has been a hard one. You have no idea how many times I would sit down to write and a week later I would realize that what I had written was for my healing but maybe not for others to read. So God used this experience to bring healing to my worn-out soul. So get out your notebook and begin to write. When I first started I went to a beautiful spot by a creek and took my notebook and began to write what I was feeling about where I had been. It was quiet there and I could think. Even if you never show another human being, it will be good for you.

If you plan on sharing your experience with a small group or a large group, then begin to type it out on the computer. Read it and pray over it a few days, then go back to it. See if God shows you anything you need to change. When you are finished, get on your knees and thank God for your *thus far* experience and ask Him to use it to bring encouragement to another who needs to hear what you have been through. What may seem nothing to you may be just what someone else needs to hear.

When you are ready, speak to your group leader and tell them you would like to share your story. Don't let satan tell you your story is crazy and no one would want to hear it. Everyone has a story of something they have come through and everyone has importance and meaning. We need to remember God never brings meaningless trials into our lives. So use this time to open up and share.

You may say, "I am not a public speaker!" No one is born into the role of being a public speaker. Now some are more comfortable than others in front of people, but you can do it. God calls each of us to stand up and say a word for Him. He tells us in His Word that He will give us what we need. All He needs is a willing heart.

GOD WILL SPEAK THROUGH YOU

God will speak through you and help you tell your story. When Peter went out to preach, one reason the people believed was because they knew Peter and knew he was uneducated. He basically had not been to seminary, yet he was teaching the people as an expert. They knew only Jesus could give him the power to speak with boldness and confidence. Jesus will do the same thing for you and me. You will never know how God could use your story to touch another until you open up and share it.

In class I heard a story I will never forget. A young lady came to our class to share about her passion for Hope House International. She appeared nervous at first but was passionate about this ministry. She then began to share why she was so passionate about helping them. As she told us her story I felt tears stream down my face. It was hard for her and she wept as she shared what she had been through. She touched every woman in that room with her story. I will never forget what she shared that day. She is now writing a book about her life and I can't wait to read it. What she has been through *thus far* is agonizing, yet God is using her past for His good.

So I want to encourage you today to share your story. You never know what impact you might have on someone's life if you never share. So many days satan tries to discourage me by telling me not to open my mouth; it will do more harm than good to share about my life. At those times I am tempted to do what we were taught and sweep it under the carpet and never speak of it again. Then I remember that in God's Word I am to go out and share what He has done in my life, the good and the bad. I am to share how he takes my mess and makes it a work of art. That involves sharing the junk in a way that will help someone else and let them know they aren't alone. So know there is someone who needs to hear what you have to say.

LEADING A BIBLE STUDY

Maybe you could start a Bible study in your home and each month let someone just share their *thus far* experiences. Several years ago, God allowed me to lead a women's conference. As I prayed He began to place certain women on my heart. I went to each at different times and ask them if they would pray about sharing something in their life on video that we could show during our conference. It could be their salvation experience, anything. I told them I felt that God wanted to use them during this weekend. The day we went to the church to video their testimonies we all came together in a circle to pray. I will never forget as each one called out to God in prayer for each other the power I felt in that circle of prayer. God used each of them in a powerful way during the conference. Everyone was touched by their testimonies.

Pray and ask God to help you to be able to share from your heart about your journey with Christ. I love to hear people's stories of where they have been and what God has brought them through. It warms my heart to hear from other people. He will bless you and use your story in ways you can't imagine.

Get out your journals and begin to write! Get on your knees and ask God to give you a place to share your story. Then gather a group of friends and begin to pray for wisdom and for God to use it in ways only He can. A few weeks before you are going to speak share your story with a friend. This will allow you to feel at ease at telling your *thus far* journey in front of someone else. You can do this, tell yourself that every day.

I can't wait to hear your stories. I want you to email me or get on my website and share your story with me. I am excited for you. Remember God uses ordinary people to do extraordinary things! So get busy and start writing today! Your story is valuable in God's eyes. I love you my friends. Your *thus far* journey has purpose, so let God use you today.

Today Lord, I can't say Your Name out loud
I have no strength, this storm is overtaking me
I Know Your Word has promised, to make firm the weak; but I can't see
Your plan, and I'm too weak to stand.

I'm in the eye of the storm, I see the waves crashing down on me; this time
they're too strong, all hope seems gone
Then suddenly I feel Your arms surrounding me; I'm still in the storm, but
not alone
My God is holding on to me.

When you pass through the waters, I will be with you; and when You walk
through the fire, you will not burned
Nor will the flames even scorch you, or the rivers overflow you; for I am the
Lord Your God, and I will walk with you.

You're in the eye of the storm, you feel the waves crashing down on you;
this time they're too strong, all hope seems gone
But my child I have My arms surrounding you; Your still in the storm, but
not alone;
I am holding on to you.
You have promised never to leave or forsake me, I'm your child; so even
though this storm still rages, I'll keep my eyes on the rock of ages, I know
victory will come.

Words and music written by Tammy Daniel

VERSES TO HELP YOU ON YOUR JOURNEY

I have included many scriptures in these chapters to help you. I decided to list some of them back here as well. Many friends would send me a text with a verse in it or a card. I still look at those when I need a boost. I would journal many of those verses each day. So I hope these help you as they have been a great source of strength for me. Many of these verses are on index cards on my refrigerator, on my mirror in my bathroom, and above my kitchen sink. These are the places I am the most, so I have placed these cards where I will constantly be faced with the truth I need to live in victory.

When you feel overwhelmed and anxious, God reminds you to rest in Him.
From the end of the earth I will cry to You, When my heart is overwhelmed;
Lead me to the rock that is higher than I. Psalm 61:2
Cast all your anxiety on Him because He cares for you. I Peter 5:7
When my spirit was overwhelmed within me, You knew my path. Psalm 142:3
Rest in the Lord and wait patiently for Him. Psalm 37:7

When your problems seem too big for God to handle, God says to stand still and trust Him
You have armed me with strength for the battle... Psalm 18:39
Thou art my hiding place; thou shall preserve me from trouble; thou will compass me about with songs of deliverance. Psalm 32:7
Stand still and see the salvation of the Lord, which He will accomplish for you today. Exodus 14:13
Be strong, and of good courage, do not be afraid, nor be dismayed, for the Lord your God is with you wherever you go. Joshua 1:1

When You don't believe God hears you when you pray, God reminds you that He not only hears you but He will deliver you

The righteous cry out, and the Lord hears them; He delivers them from all their troubles. The Lord is close to the brokenhearted and saves those who are crushed in spirit. Psalm 34:17-18

Now this confidence we have in Him, that if we ask anything according to His will, He hears us. And if we know He hears us, whatever we ask, we know that we have the petitions that we have asked of Him. I John 5:14

Do not cast away your confidence, which has great reward. For you have need of endurance, so that after you have done the will of God, you may receive the promise. (hang in there) Hebrews 10:35-36

When You don't have have the strength to go on, God says I will be your strength

I can do all things through Christ who strengths me. Philippians 4:13

He gives power to the weak, and to those who have no might He increases strength. Isaiah 40:29

God is our refuge and strength, a very present help in trouble. Psalm 46:1

He drew me out of many waters, He delivered me from my strong enemy, from those who hated me. For they were too strong for me, they confronted me in the day of my calamity, but the Lord was my support. He also brought me out into a broad place; He delivered me because He delighted in me! Psalm 18:16-19

Strengthen the weak hands. And make firm the feeble knees. Say to those who are fearful-hearted, Be strong, do not fear! Behold your God will come with a vengeance, with the recompense of God; He will come and save you. Isaiah 35:3-4

When your suffering seems to have no end, God reminds you He has a perfect plan, you can endure with your hand in His

Beloved, do not think it strange concerning the fiery trial which is to try you, as though some strange thing happened to you; but rejoice to the extent that you partake of Christ's sufferings, that when His glory is revealed, you may also be glad with exceeding joy. I Peter 4:12

When you pass through the waters, I will be with you; and through the rivers, they shall not overflow you. When you walk through, the fire, you shall not be burned, nor shall the flame scorch you. For I am the Lord your God. Isaiah 43:2-3

When the past keeps coming to the front of your mind, God says I will take those thoughts captive
You will keep him in perfect peace, whose mind is stayed on You! Isaiah 26:3
One thing I do, forgetting those things which are behind me and reaching forward to those things which are ahead, I press toward the goal for the prize of the upward call of God in Christ Jesus. Philippians 3:13-14
Do not remember the former things, nor consider the things of old. Behold, I will do a new thing, now it shall spring forth; shall you not know it? I will even make a road in the wilderness and rivers in the desert. Isaiah 43:18

When doubt and fears arise within you, God reminds you He will always be faithful to you
The steadfast love of the Lord never ceases, his mercies never come to an end; they are new every morning, great is His faithfulness. Lamentations 3:22-23
Psalm 138 and 139. Read every word!
Some trust in chariots, and horses; but we will remember the name of the Lord our God. Psalm 20:7
Call upon Me in the day of trouble; I will deliver you, and you shall glorify Me. Psalm 50:15
Whenever I am afraid, I will trust in You. Psalm 56:3

When you don't think you can forgive another, God says I forgave you
Therefore as an elect of God, holy and beloved, put on tender mercies, kindness, humility, meekness, longsuffering; bearing with one another, and forgiving one another, if anyone has a complaint against another, even as Christ forgave you, so you also must do. Colossians 3:12-13

And be kind to one another, tenderhearted, forgiving one another, even as God in Christ forgave you. Ephesians 4:32

ACKNOWLEDGMENTS

My family and friends have been hearing me say for the past few years, "I am going to get my book ready soon." I know they all thought "soon" would never come, and they became sick of hearing me talk about it. Well, guess what everyone? I am done. Praise God I am completely done! You don't have to hear me talk about the "what if's", and "Can you read this and see if it makes sense?" I am done writing my story!

I want to thank my wonderful Lord for seeing me through writing this book. During the final days, satan fought me every step of the way, but my God is greater than any force satan can throw my way. Thank you, my Heavenly Father, for Your strength and love. Without You I am nothing.

Thank you to my family. Marcus (and his wife Abbie), Cole, Victoria, and Emma, you are amazing children. I am blessed beyond measure that God saw fit to make me your mother. Your love for each other and Jesus stands out to everyone who meets you. Thank you for your love and allowing me to write my story and share it with the world. I love watching how God is using you, and can't wait to continue to watch your lives unfold.

To my girlfriends, you are amazing. Priscilla, you have encouraged me daily for months without end. I can't thank you enough for your love and support. Judy, Stacey, Leeza, Marcheta, Lisa, Andrea, Jacky, Leanna, Barb, Margaret, Vickie, Maggie, and Cindy, thank you all for listening to all my junk and still loving me. You have walked with me through the hardest storms of my life. I can never thank you all for your encouragement, laughs, listening ears, and for just loving me when I was unlovable. You are the best friends a girl could ever have. I love you all and thank you for everything. I love doing life with you.

To Marcia Lavely, who read these pages many times. I know she prayed I would not change or add anything else. She took my manuscript and whipped it into shape. Thank you for your countless hours of reading and correcting.

Also, Barbara Cheney, who did the final edit. Thank you so much!

To my friend Debbie, thank you for staying up till the wee hours of the morning as I read and you helped me open up and share more of my heart with these readers than I expected to. You have been such a great help to me during these last few months. You helped me make my story come to life. I'm so thankful for your help.

To my ex-husband, thank you for allowing me to share our story with the world. I am grateful that we have remained friends through all of this. Some people think our relationship is strange, but I am thankful we can be such good friends. It is a blessing as we continue to raise our children.

My mom was so excited that God had brought me through so much and I was writing a book. She was so proud of me. She encouraged me every step of the way. She always told me to hold my head up high and just trust God to carry me through. Whenever I came to her and didn't know what to do, she encouraged me to just pray and wait for God. When mom could hardly walk, she continued to go to church, carrying her oxygen as she walked down the aisle. She loved the Lord with all her heart. Six months ago my mom ran through the gates of heaven. She taught me so much in her final days of life. She is my hero. I pray to be half the woman she was. I am so proud to be her daughter. Heaven is sweeter with you there mom.

I am so thankful to have completed this task I know God asked me to do. I am so thankful to be His vessel. It's amazing to think He desires to use each one of us to do His work. May each word I speak, write, and sing always bring glory to His Almighty Name!

Tammy Daniel is a speaker, worship leader, pianist, and author.

Her favorite role is being a mother to her four children. Her passion Is sharing Jesus through her story to help others find hope and healing.

You can write to her at: **PO Box 452**
Burns, TN 37029

Or email her through her website: www.tammydaniel.com

Facebook: Tammy Daniel

"We have been blessed on many occasions to have Tammy Daniel minister to our congregation by serving as our pianist and providing special music. She is both an accomplished musician and vocalist. Each time, her playing and vocal renderings have been nothing short of awe-inspiring and have added immeasurably to our worship experience. Her talents are great gifts and she is always ready to employ them to bring glory to her Lord. Members of our church look forward to those times she can be with us and they leave worship having been to the mountaintop."
Rev. Robert D. Truitt, Pastor
Cumberland Presbyterian Church
Dickson, Tennessee

"Any woman who desires to embrace the future with hope will appreicate the ministry of my friend, Tammy. Her life story will inspire hurting women to overcome strongholds and learn to walk in obedience and victory. God uses her messages in song and her powerful testimony to touch hearts. She is a true spiritual gem."
Judy Overton

"Tammy is a talented daughter of the King who is passionately following His voice in her life. Her message will most definitely direct you to the heart of God."
Leighann McCoy
Author/Speaker